The Power of Self-Imaging

Joel D Johnson

G. RANDALL PUBLISHING CO.
1505 N. Groveland Ave.
Longview, TX 75601

Copyrighted © 2016 Joel D Johnson

All rights reserved.
No part of this book may be reproduced or transmitted in any form or by any means, electronic or mechanical, including photocopying, recording, or by any information storage and retrieval system, except in the case of brief quotations used in book reviews and critical articles, without the permission in writing from the author or the publisher.

Library of Congress Cataloging-in-Publication Data
Johnson, Joel D. 1936
The Power of Self-Imaging: Who am I? What am I? Why am I here?
1. Self-help 2. Personal Growth 3. Spiritual
4. Johnson, Joel D., 2016
p. cm.
ISBN: 0965943917
ISBN No. 9780965943918 (alk. paper)

Cover design by Audrey Knight

Manufactured in the United States of America

The best way to become acquainted with a subject is write a book about it.

—**Benjamin Disraeli**

Every human being, like all of nature, will only find its strength and power to transform and grow from the Spirit of the Universe that exists within its self. Seeking enlightenment out there somewhere will only bring frustration and disappointment.

—**Joel D. Johnson**

Dedication

I dedicate this book to my wife, Louise, the love of my life, my best friend and life partner, who has remained by my side, supporting me through thick and thin, and to our four children, their spouses and our nine fantastic grandchildren. I love you more than you will ever know.

Acknowledgements

TO THOSE WHO, as a favor to me, read the manuscript and added their suggestions in an effort to help make this book more readable, thank you.

Special thanks go to my friend Gayle Wilkening Poland for her editing expertise and for her tireless effort to keep my rambling mind focused. Thanks to Audrey Knight for her ideas and design of the book cover.

I give all the glory and praise to the Spirit of the Universe that lives within each of us; I am most grateful. Without your inspired words this book could not exist.

Disclaimer

I MAKE NO claims of being a physicist, a PhD, a neurologist, psychiatrist, psychologist, medical doctor, witch doctor, guru, or cult leader.

The information contained in this book is derived from my many years of scientific and biblical study, human observation, and mental programming. This book was written with the intent to share what I have learned through my walk in self-discovery. It is meant for personal growth and spiritual enlightenment purposes only.

I have made every effort to give proper citation for the ideas and works of other's knowledge used in this book. If I have failed in any way to give proper credit, it is not my intent, and I sincerely apologize.

Along with the publisher, we make no guarantees or warranties as to results you may personally achieve by exploring and practicing in whole or part the contents of this book.

Whether lives change for the better due to the contents of this book, I cannot say. I only know it works for me.

Review

WHAT YOU DO determines your future. Your actions are in your hands.

There are hidden forces within the mind forged during the painful moments of our past. These forces tend to constrain what we see as possible. Yet, there ever exists the possibility of choice.

Accurate self-knowledge is power. If you want power and mastery, get a good owner's manual. I stand in awe of Joel's honesty, determination, courage, and hard-won wisdom. The Power of Self-Imaging is both a philosopher's tome and a practical manual for redefining and honing who you are, giving you more power, freedom, self-expression, and peace of mind.

—**Frank S. Murphy, D.O., Psychiatrist,
Author of** *Power Without Pills*

Table of Contents

Dedication	vii
Acknowledgements	ix
Disclaimer	xi
Review	xiii
Introduction	xix
Why This Book	xx
The Beginning	xx
Courage to Write	xxi
Mind/Brain Concept	xxiii
Acceptance	xxv
Please Note	xxvi
1 The Illusion	1
2 Self-Discovery	4
You are More Than a Form	6
3 Perception/Interpretation	11
My Stories	11
4 Mental Baggage	20
Ego	22
Servant of the Mind	23
Decompress and Forgive	24

5	Self-Talk	26
6	Beginning the Process	29
	Making This Work for You	30
	Wanting, Needing and Having	31
	How to Create an Affirmation	32
	Desperation	33
	Affirmation 1	36
7	Secrets of the Heart	37
	Change Requires Integrity	38
	Affirming the Desires of Your Heart	42
	Affirmation 2	44
8	Faith to Believe	45
	The I Can't Disease	47
	Affirmation – Belief - Faith – Action	49
	Affirmation 3	51
9	Mental Hard Drive	52
	Kicking Sand	53
	Dale Carnegie	56
	The One-Minute Speech	58
	The Setup	59
	Affirmation 4	61
10	It Starts on the Inside	62
	Wishing and Dreaming	65
	Living in a Dream World	66
	God Knows Your Secrets	67
	Voices in Our Head	67
	Affirmation 5	70
11	The Comfort Zone	71
	The Life of John	72
	How to Train a Flea	73
	Affirmation 6	76
12	Choices	77
	Books of Gold	80
	Brainstorming	82
	Affirmation 7	85

13	Suppression/Compression and Sensory Reality	86
	Affirmation 8	90
14	The Power of Affirmations	91
	Your Move	93
	Affirmation 9	94
15	Affirming Your Dream	95
	Being Specific	97
	Good Advice	100
	Confess It to Possess It	101
	Affirmation 10	102
16	Imagination and the Mind	103
	The Dream	103
	Affirmation 11	110
17	I Think I Am	111
	Our Changing Philosophy	112
	Education and the Workplace	113
	An Education at the Swimming Hole	115
	The Cat's Meow	117
	The Missing Quarter	121
	Affirmation 12	134
18	A View in the Mirror	135
	Transformation	136
	Mind-to-Mind	137
	Judging the Cover	137
	Affirmation 13	139
19	Self-Acceptance	140
	Consciousness	143
	Affirmation 14	144
20	The Formless Dimension	145
	Sensory Reality	146
	Coming to Grips	147
	Affirmation 15	150
21	Eliminating Bad Habits	151
	Losing Weight	160
	Affirmation 16	163

| 22 | Eliminating Fear | 164 |
| 23 | The Final Analysis | 169 |

About the Author 173
Resources 175

Introduction

The unseen world is the real world, and when we are willing to explore the unseen levels of our bodies, we can tap in to the immense creative power that lies at our source.

—Deepak Chopra, M.D

IN THE MIDST of my research into self-discovery, I stumbled upon universal secrets that until then were unknown to me. These scientific and spiritual secrets that I experienced and continue to experience function as an entity in a separate dimension within.

I believe, though hundreds of authors have written on this subject in various genres for centuries, very few people really know or understand this separate dimension. Very few authors have observed this powerful life force; thus, I express this personal discovery as *universal secrets*, secret's of the mind, body and soul.

This life force within us is one with the Spirit of the Universe and is the observer of all things within the context of our life, both real and imagined. It acts with powerful energy that is aligned with all that is or will ever be.

You may have already observed the power of this entity within yourself through your own personal experience. At the time of my discovery I was totally unaware of its existence and its amazing power.

• • •

WHY THIS BOOK
This book was written because I believe there are few people who realize or will acknowledge the scientific and spiritual truths that exist within this seemingly hidden dimension. This is a dimension that requires deeper understanding through dissecting the physical, spiritual, and scientific elements. It is a reality so powerful that it is sure to change your life forever, as it has mine. It will, at the very least, expose the mind to a new dimension within. Once this dimension is observed the mind will surely never return to its original state.

• • •

THE BEGINNING
I earnestly began seeking answers and making changes in my own life in 1953 when I was a sophomore in high school. My awareness and personal transformation began when I first grasped a small inkling of the possibility that such a dimension within me could be a reality. It was a weird feeling, an experience that made me wonder what was going on within my foggy brain.

It was during this time that I began to realize I had literally existed from day to day in a mental fog, which had blurred my thinking and was keeping me from reaching my true potential as a student and as a human being.

On that fall day, September 1953, while combing my hair in the high school men's room, I looked in the mirror and sensed my self beyond the body, intact, yet separated, as though I was seeing two different entities. As though a separate person on the inside of me was observing the reflection of my body in the mirror, I stood there for several minutes sensing something inside myself was observing the reflection. I could not see the entity within me that was observing the reflected image, but I was totally aware of its existence.

On that day that the mental fog slowly began to lift from my mind, I realized for the first time that I am not alone and that this something inside me is watching my thoughts, my actions, my reactions, and my attitude. It knows me better than I know myself. I then realized I could no longer hide my thoughts or deeds from this entity within.

This point of realization was not an out-of-body experience, nor was it a sudden transformation. It was a transformation that continues even to this day as I seek to understand more fully the lessons I have learned from that event and from many years of research since.

• • •

COURAGE TO WRITE

This book did not easily flow from my mind as I hoped it would. I struggled with the idea of writing it for many years, fearing rejection, while nursing a poor self-image and believing I was unqualified as a writer. During those many years of self-doubt, I let the idea of writing this book and exposing my own personal life experiences set on my mental shelf. How was I to explain a separate entity that is alive and well within each of us?

After my transformational experience in 1953, along with extensive research and study, my desire to write this book became stronger in 1984. Regardless of my less than perfect writing skills, I had to do it. I had no choice. I was helplessly drawn to it.

I dreaded the thought of having to do the necessary research involved. It meant reading and studying more books, talking to experts, searching for scientific fact, and philosophical and spiritual answers, not to mention reprogramming and exposing my own mind to numerous new findings. Nonetheless, I could not turn loose of the thoughts that seemed to dominate my mind. For whatever reason,

I recognize now that writing this book is one of the requirements for fulfilling my preordained purpose in life and for my own piece of mind.

It was a crazy idea. It was going to be very hard work, and it has been. I thought, "Who would read it? Would writing this book really help anyone?" I thought of every excuse possible, but something pushed me into a corner and took them all away.

As I began to do the necessary research, I realized that the seemingly insignificant personal stories I had created about my life and who I thought I was were derived from unfounded interpretations of traumatic events and negative mental programming that happened during my early childhood. Through deeper study I realized my perceptions of those events and my personal interpretations were mostly false.

It was during that time of personal discovery that I experienced a turning point and was mentally released from the anger and guilt that had consumed me for most of my life. I finally grasped the realization that the emotions I felt and carried with me from childhood were self-imposed. The self-image I had nurtured all my life was not who I am at all.

It dawned on me that millions of other people like me are holding on to a false self-image as well—a self-image that has been manufactured by their imagination and fueled by the false interpretations of their own poorly perceived events. Often those inaccurate self-authored stories cause people to feel as I felt: inadequate, angry, afraid, lonely, frustrated, fraudulent, sad, and empty.

The process of writing this book has been more challenging than I first imagined it would be. It has been a long journey of self-discovery coupled with much difficulty grasping things that at first appeared unreal. As the truth was exposed, I sometimes felt as though I was a character in the 1960's TV series, *The Twilight Zone.*

• • •

MIND/BRAIN CONCEPT

As I began to dig deep inside myself, fighting all the way, but determined to understand what I was feeling and experiencing, I dug deep into books on how the brain functions, behavior motivation, human relations, and spiritual foundation. I studied the Bible and talked to experts. I studied how humans relate, and what underlies spiritual growth. Over the years I accumulated a library of books on these subjects. I became passionate. I wanted to know.

One of the more difficult things for me to comprehend was the fact that the human brain and the mind are not one and the same. Contrary to popular belief, the brain is the servant of the mind. The brain is grey matter where billions of neurons exist. It is the machinery of the nervous system and, of course, necessary for mental and physical function.

The mind is energy. Energy is not matter. Energy works on and through matter. Energy cannot be created or destroyed, but it can be transformed. The brain and body are mobilized through transformed energy. It is this mental and physical energy that is designed and was created to carry out the wishes of the Universal Mind.

I learned that while you do not have to think for your automatic body functions to work, your mind can control some of them when focused thinking is applied. With total concentration, you can raise or lower your blood pressure, slow your breathing, increase or decrease your heart rate, and increase or decrease your body temperature. Through concentration your mind can cause the brain to focus on any given area of the body, releasing anxieties, anger, and much more.

Other astonishing discoveries had me wondering if anything in my perceived world was actually real at all. I learned that we are not who or what we see in the mirror. We are much more than can be observed or understood through our sensory system alone. We also tend to confuse our own reality with mental programming that has been consciously and subliminally embedded in the deepest recesses of our subconscious mind.

Unaware of the observer within the physical form, we often emulate people we believe represent and embody the personality and character we would like to adopt for ourselves. In reality, we could never become like any other person because we are unique individuals in design, mind, and spirit.

> **Man's goings are of the LORD; how can a man then understand his own way?**
>
> **—Proverbs 20:24**

• • •

REASON FOR BEING

Scientific research, study, and analysis prove that everything in the universe has its place and reason for being. You were conceived and born for a purpose, a great preordained missions that only you could accomplish. This is true for every plant, animal, mineral, all matter, and atoms in the universe. Everything in the universe, known and unknown, has its purpose for being.

It may be that we were born to serve as an example of how to live life to its fullest, or it may be that we were born to serve as an example of what *not* to do. It may be that we were born to achieve great things, become extremely wealthy and change the world, or it may be that it is our destiny to live our life in mediocrity or in total desperation and poverty. It could also mean that our purpose is to influence the life of others in such a unique way that it will in turn change the world for the good of all mankind.

Like it or not, we, like all plants, animals, minerals, matter, and atoms within the universe are consistently moving toward our preordained life purpose. The results, like ripples in the water, will touch the world, teaching and enriching all life forms.

The way you have turned out being as a person—how you have lived your life through thought and action—is the way you were meant to turn out being. The way you continue to turn out being is part of the universal formula for all things working together for good. There is no way you can change it or escape it. What is...is! When change manifests itself in your life, it was meant to be. It was preordained to occur in you at that specific point in time.

The thoughts we believe are our own is energy flowing from the universal mind and is not our own. We are spirit beings experiencing life in a physical form we call our body. We are beacons of light in a world of mental darkness. Our path is preordained. We cannot fail.

And the Lord God formed man of the dust of the ground, and breathed into his nostrils the breath of life; and man became a <u>living soul</u>.

—Genesis 2: 7

Included in the universal formula for all things working together for good is your strong desire to discover your reason for being, your real purpose for living, who you are, and what you are. Keep in mind your reason for being is not *out there somewhere*. It is on the inside of you. Once you discover this dimension within, you will discover your own reason for being. Through self-discovery, acceptance, and change, you will find and understand your preordained purpose in life.

• • •

ACCEPTANCE
Existing as social animals absorbed with life and living, we have a deep desire to be accepted and loved. We want to know that our life is important, not only to ourselves, but to others as well. We want to be respected and appreciated, and we will go to great lengths to achieve that goal.

The desire for acceptance, respect, and love is so strong that we tend to surround ourselves with people and things that at first seem to satisfy that desire; however, with the most elaborate praise and prestige there is often a feeling of emptiness inside that seems to make us feel incomplete. I have come to believe the empty feeling inside is caused by the lingering desire to know: who am I, what am I, and why am I here.

The *Power of Self-Imaging* is about self-discovery, change, and helping us get in touch with our true self. It is about helping us recognize the mental baggage that has held us back. It is about helping us get more in sync with the hidden entities within us. It is about recognizing the powers within that want us to succeed and those that want us to fail.

My belief is that you will not find your purpose in life until you recognize the entities within, the entities that hold the key to the door for your life-purpose and true happiness.

While sensing your true self, you will recognize the never-ending mental chatter that stands guard over the door that contains the lock that opens the door to your preordained future. Through negative mental chatter (self-talk) we are locked in, unable to understand, but through positive self-talk we begin to see clearly and the door is opened. You choose!

• • •

PLEASE NOTE
As you know, for the process of learning to work, repetition is vital. You can't expect to learn, to a higher degree, without dedication and consistent practice. Ask any champion. Realizing the importance of *getting it*, I have purposely repeated many key points and stressed them in various forms for your benefit.

I was preordained to write this book and you were preordained to read it. Not everyone is. You are special.

1
The Illusion

People like us who believe in physics know that the distinction between the past, the present and the future is only a stubbornly persistent illusion.

—Attributed to Albert Einstein

TO UNDERSTAND WHO you are, what you are, and why you are here, you must first understand that in reality you only experience your own existence one nanosecond at a time in the consciousness of your own mind. Your perception and interpretation of reality, your own experiences, and what you believe to be true about yourself and your environment, only exists within your own brain. As a human being, without consciousness there can be no reality.

Perception and interpretation of what you believe to be real in the context of your mind is the result of conscious and unconscious thought. The interpretation of the stories you continually enhance and tell yourself about the person you believe you have turned out being is an illusionary mental concept created by constant mental chatter and mental programming.

The mental concept or picture of the person you believe to be your *self* is stored in your subconscious. This picture is derived from what you think you know about yourself, your world, and the environment that you occupy.

It is not the things we think we know that we know that do the most damage. It is the things we know, but don't know that we know, that have the potential to do a lifetime of mental and physical damage.

Some events hidden away in our subconscious are so traumatic that the brain automatically suppresses them without conscious permission. Many events, such as pain from labor at childbirth, the loss of a limb, traumatic head injuries that rendered a state of unconsciousness, or traumatic shock received from various accidents or witnessed at the scene of trauma, are often suppressed. These suppressed memories, supposedly un-recallable, forgotten, and dismissed from our mind, remain locked away in the depths of our subconscious.

Other experiences that have been consciously compressed are things we can recall and would suppress if we could. They include things we don't want to think about because they are too painful, secrets that we've hidden away in the back of our mental closet, hoping no one will ever find out about. We imagine that once exposed, this information would make us look bad to those we love, and to those with whom we choose to associate.

Some personal stories we have mindfully created, we designed to make us look good. These stories serve to justify our egotistical nature as we tell others about the person we imagine to be. These edited stories, repeated in our mind over and over, each time enhanced, eventually keep us from recognizing any resemblance to the person we have turned out being. Who then am "I"?

Eckhart Tolle, in his book, *A New Earth, says,* " "I" embodies the primordial error, a misperception of who you are, an illusory sense of identity. This is ego. This illusory sense of self is what Albert Einstein referred to as "an optical illusion of consciousness."

THE POWER OF SELF-IMAGING

Ken Weber's says, in his book, *Integral Psychology, Consciousness, Spirit, Psychology, Therapy*, "If you get a sense of yourself right now, simply notice what it is that you call "you" —you might notice at least two parts to this "self": one, there is some sort of observing self (an inner subject or watcher, and two, some objective things that you can see or know about yourself."

If I could, I would love to touch my finger on your forehead and re-program your subconscious, instantly expelling those hidden secrets and dissolving those mental illusions that have interrupted the fullness of a fantastic life that you so rightly deserve. I would love to wave a wand and somehow instantly make you consciously aware of what your life purpose is, what you are, who you really are (the one you have been seeking all your life), but that is not possible. YOU, however, hold the key that unlocks your subconscious and the inner *power* that is available to you. It is this power, hidden so deep within you that you may not realize you have access to that will awaken you.

You have the power to open yourself up to new possibilities that are preordained and available to you. To do this, you must seek the key—the key to change. You cannot change if you fear change. You cannot grow as a person without faith and belief that you can change. Change requires deeper and deeper awareness of what you are, who you are, and the real purpose for your life.

And I say unto you, Ask, and it shall be given you; seek, and ye shall find; knock, and it shall be opened unto you.

—Holy Bible- Luke 11:9

2
Self-Discovery

What lies behind us, and what lies before us are tiny matters compared to what lies within us.

—**Ralph Waldo Emerson/Albert Jay Nock**

THE FIRST STEP toward change is self-discovery. It is not only about being in the hunt to discover your real identity it is also about becoming aware of the hidden dimensions within. Self-discovery requires an open mind and the willingness to examine the illusions that you have created for yourself.

Self-image is the mental concept or image of the person you have created as your "self". It is the person you believe you are, the image of "me" now stored away in your subconscious mind. Yet, that mental image that you truly believe to be "I" or "me" may be false. The image of yourself that you have implanted in your subconscious mind might be based on the person you believe others think you are and not who you really are.

Self-image is the mental picture or subconscious perception of the person you think is "I" or "me". Self-esteem is how you *feel* about

THE POWER OF SELF-IMAGING

the person you think you are. Self-esteem is an emotion. A good self-esteem is the feeling that you hold in your mind that you are worthy and have self-respect. Poor self-esteem is a feeling that you are not worthy and have little self-respect; "I'm no good".

The development of your self-image and self-esteem began at birth. As a baby you had no concept of "I", "me," "mine", or "self". When you were a baby you were basically consumed with hunger, comfort, and after a period of time, your body.

As you grew you began to sense your world around you—the world that appears to exist outside the brain and body. After a couple of years you began to comprehend body language and a few words. Soon you were trying hard to live up to what you believed your parents, siblings, and society expected of you. While trying to live up to everyone else's expectations you may have become confused concerning your own identity.

Through your own observation, mental programming and self-talk, you have created a mental picture of the person you now believe is the "I", "me," and "self", the person you believe you are. In most cases this mental picture you hold in your subconscious mind is based on your perception and interpretation of the person you believe others want you to be, rather than the person you really are.

It is in those formative years, ages one through seven, that you absorbed things like a sponge. You absorbed things based on what you imagined to be true about your self and our environment instead of actually facts. The information stored in the subconscious mind during those formative years formed what you perceived to be "me", "myself" and what you believed to be your real world.

What you consciously thought (and most likely continue to think) of as "myself" during those formative years, established the basic mental picture of the person you hold in your subconscious mind. And unless you choose to change the concept of who you have become, you will hold this view of "me" the rest of your life.

> *You act, and feel, not according to what things are really like, but according to the image your mind holds of what they are like.*
>
> —Maxwell Maltz, M.D., F.I.C.S.

How you interpret what you believe to be the truth about your life's experiences will be the determining factor as to how you will turn out being and acting as a person. You will act on the interpretations of what you perceive as real and true. Those actions become your reality.

You cannot change the past and what is now only a memory. How you interpret what you have learned will result in how you conduct your life and will play an important part in how you perceive what you believe to be your future. How you conduct your life, that is, how you are being and acting as a human being, becomes your perception of "what is."

• • •

YOU ARE MORE THAN A FORM

In the process of discovering the person you really are and what you are, you need to understand that you are more than a human form. This process will require an investigation into what Einstein called "the unseen world".

According to the Apostle Paul, the human form is only temporary. If that is true, what happens to you when you die?

The Apostle Paul, in the *Holy Bible*, writes to the church of Corinth; 2nd Corinthians-5:1–5 (Italics are my own for emphasis.)

> For we know that when this earthly tent *we live in* is taken down (that is, when we die and *leave this earthly body*), we will have a house in heaven, an eternal body made for us by God himself and not by human hands. We grow weary in our present bodies, and we long to put on our heavenly bodies

like new clothing. For we will put on *heavenly bodies; we will not be spirits without bodies.* While we live in these earthly bodies, we groan and sigh, but it's not that we want to die and get rid of *these bodies that clothe us.* Rather, we want to put on our new bodies so that these dying bodies will be swallowed up by life. God himself has prepared us for this, and *as a guarantee he has given us his Holy Spirit.*

According to Paul, for those that believe, God has given His Holy Spirit, the very essence of God Himself within us, making us one with Him, and He in us, the Spirit of the Universe.

God is not a human being, though He can take on human form as He did in the form of Jesus and as He has within you. He is spirit. God is the Spirit of the Universe. He is everywhere and in everything. God is in you and you are in Him. You are one with God for eternity. You are the "I", the observer, one with the great "I am," an eternal spirit being, experiencing life in a temporary form. That is who you really are, a living spirit in a dimension beyond form, experiencing life as consciousness.

Heaven is God's domain. According to the dictionary, heaven is where God lives and it is where the angels and righteous live after one dies. Where is this heaven, this Kingdom of God? According to Jesus, the Kingdom of God is within us.

> **And when Jesus was demanded of the Pharisees, when the kingdom of God should come, Jesus answered them and said, The kingdom of God cometh not with observation: Neither shall they say, Lo here or, Lo there! For behold, the kingdom of God is within you.**
>
> *— Holy Bible,* **Luke 17: 20-21**

NOTE: *Jesus said, "For behold, the kingdom of God is within you." Where then does God live? God lives within you. He is the observer in* you. He is the "I" in "I Am." He is one in you and you are one in Him. He is with you always.

Let's consider what other religions say about what happens after death.

ISLAM

The spirit is the seed from which a higher form of life grows within man, higher than physical life, just as the body has developed from a small 'seed'. Just as in the world around us higher forms of life evolve from lower ones, similarly from the life of the individual in this world is evolved his higher 'spiritual' life. During his life, man's deeds shape and mold his spirit, for better or worse, according to his deeds. When a person dies, the physical body is finished, but the spirit remains, as he or she had molded it by their deeds when alive. That is the life after death.

JUDAISM

The creation of man testifies to the eternal life of the soul. The Torah says, "And the Almighty formed the man of dust from the ground, and He blew into his nostrils the SOUL of life." (Genesis 2:7). On this verse, the Zohar states that "one who blows, blows from within himself," indicating that the soul is actually part of God's essence. Since God's essence is completely spiritual and non-physical, it is impossible that the soul should die. (The commentator Chizkuni says, this is why the verse calls it "soul of LIFE.")

That's what King Solomon meant when he wrote, "The dust will return to the ground as it was, and the spirit will return to God who gave it. (Ecclesiastes 12:17)

For anyone who believes in a just and caring God, the existence of an afterlife makes logical sense.

THE POWER OF SELF-IMAGING

BUDDHISM

In the teaching of the Buddha, all of us will pass away eventually as a part in the natural process of birth, old-age and death and that we should always keep in mind the impermanence of life, the life that we all cherish and wish to hold on.

To Buddhism, however, death is not the end of life, it is merely the end of the body we inhabit in this life, but our spirit will still remain and seek out through the need of attachment, attachment to a new body and new life.

Eve Wilson, spiritual teacher and contributor to *Mind, Body Spirit Guide,* a monthly paper, describes who you are:

Wherever you are, is a good place to be because you are there. You receive the greatest benefits from experiences when you remember who you are.

You are not an autoworker or a homemaker or a plumber or unemployed. You are an eternal and divine being living in a human body. Your human body, along with your emotions, mind and soul are learning to reflect your true self increasingly. You are evolving and growing into the perfect vehicle for yourself.

Wherever you are is exactly where that evolution and growth is taking place, so regard this present moment with the eye of the student…ask yourself with an open attitude and some curiosity: why did my God-self bring me here?

The non-believer argues there is no such thing as a God because he believes there is no absolute proof; therefore, God does not exist. However, with serious scientific study of nature and human existence, a little research into self-discovery and with actual observation and experience, the non-believer will have to admit that he is more than a form reflected in a mirror.

Self-discovery requires self-analysis, an examination of one's conscious and subconscious belief system, but because of a lifetime of negative mental programming some may find this difficult to believe and do. If they are asked, "Who is looking at the form in the mirror?" They will answer, "Me, of course." When asked, "Who is this "me" you speak of?" They will answer, often frustrated, "Me, myself, of course!" They continue to believe they are what they visually see in the mirror and nothing more. They don't realize that their true self exists separately from the body in a different dimension.

If asked, "Do you believe there is a God?" some people will say that God exists, but deep inside they believe He exists 'out there somewhere' or not at all.

The struggle to understand "what is" unearths deep feelings and is where self-discovery begins to take place.

In her book, Sarah Dessen, author of *What Happened to Goodbye*, shares her struggle to understand her enter most feelings as she experienced deep depression and feelings of suicide during a dark period in her life:

> Outside, the ocean was crashing, waves hitting sand, and then pulling back to sea. I thought of everything being washed away, again and again. We make such messes in this life, both accidentally and on purpose. But wiping the surface clean doesn't really make anything neater. It just masks what is below. It's only when you really dig down deep and go underground that you can see who you really are.

Self-discovery is a necessary step to self-awareness. Conscious awareness of the spirit-self, the very essence of God within, helps to make sense of an otherwise illusionary existence. What you perceive to be true and how you interpret those perceptions lead to actions that manifest your concept of "what is" within your own perceived world.

3
Perception/Interpretation

A man is not hurt so much by what happens, as by his opinion of what happens.

—**Michel De Montaigne**

SELF-DISCOVERY CAN LEAD to quite a revelation, as it did for me. Let me share from my personal experiences some of the many stories I created and told myself that helped form the false self-image I held onto for most of my life. I share these personal stories as an example of how seemingly insignificant events can affect the self-image one holds on to.

MY STORIES
* What actually happened? Reality!
One hot Sunday afternoon when I was six-years-old, my dad, two uncles, and two cousins decided to go skinny-dipping in a creek that ran through the pasture on our rented property. The creek was a couple hundred yards down a cow trail in the back of our farmhouse.

Dad told me not to follow them to the creek. I did not listen and quietly followed them anyway. To teach me obedience, he threw me in the creek, clothes and all. Dad meant no harm, and he knew I would be safe. My uncle caught me just as I went under water. Dad was only teaching me a lesson in life for my own sake. My dad truly loved me.

My perception of what happened
Dad threw me in the creek, clothes and all, hoping I would drown. I sank, but just as I went under, my uncle grabbed me and saved my life. I did not know how to swim. It scared me senseless. If my uncle had not caught me, I would have drowned.

My interpretation of what happened
My dad does not love me. He wishes I had never been born.

* What actually happened? Reality!
When I was in the second grade, my teacher and principal accused me of stealing a quarter. They said I took it from another student's coat that was hanging next to mine in the coat closet.

After what seemed to be hours of interrogation, I lied and told them I took the quarter. I told them I lost the quarter in the sand on the playground at recess. I told them I had a quarter in my piggy bank at home and I would give her my quarter.

My home was about a mile from the school, which we walked to and from daily. They sent me home and told me to bring the quarter back the following day. When I arrived home I told my mother what happened. She told my dad.

My dad had always told me to be honest and never admit to doing something that I did not do. He said, "I would die first. Admitting to something you did not do is the same is lying, and I cannot stand a liar. Do you understand me?"

He was teaching me a lesson in integrity. My dad loved me so much he wanted to make sure I was always honest to myself and to others and that I would stand my ground in any situation.

My dad punished me for lying. He spanked me in anger and then went to the school and taught the principal a lesson in human relations.

My perception of what happened
The teacher and principal are horrible human beings. They accused me of being a thief, but had no proof.

My dad spanked me because I admitted to doing something I did not do.

I was innocent.

My interpretation of what happened
Teachers and principals do not like me. My dad does not love me. They wish I had never been born.

* What actually happened? Reality!
My dad told me I would never amount to a hill of beans if I didn't pay attention to my teachers and to him. My dad and my teachers were only trying to help me.

Those words, *"You will never amount to a hill of beans,"* was his way of challenging me.

My perception of what happened
Many times my dad told me I would never amount to a hill of beans. It was his favorite line. I cannot communicate with him. He has no confidence in my ability to do anything.

My interpretation of what happened
My dad does not love me. He wishes I had never been born.

* What actually happened? Reality!
When I was a young boy my sister's cat had a litter of baby kittens. We took the kittens to the pasture to play with them. We spread a blanket and one of the kittens crawled under the blanket. Not having seen it crawl under the blanket, I accidently sat on the kitten and crushed it to death.

It was extremely upsetting to my sister and to me that I had killed the baby kitten. My sister struck out in anger—a normal human reaction. She didn't mean to hurt me with the words she said. She loves me.

My perception of what happened
I accidently sat on my sister's kitten and killed it. Her response: "You are a murderer! You are a killer and you are going to hell for killing my baby kitten." She wishes something really bad would happen to me.

My interpretation of what happened
My sister does not love me. She wishes I had never been born.

• • •

EMBELLISHED SELF-TALK
As the years passed I embellished the interpretation of those perceived events to satisfy the need to justify my feelings and to look good to those with whom I was sharing my stories.

Whenever the opportunity presented itself, I would tell *my stories*. I believed *my stories*, embellishments and all, and I believed the stories really happened the way I perceived and interpreted them. I was not aware, however, that I had absorbed and hidden away the negative interpretations in my subconscious mind. The more I told *my stories* and repeated them in my head the more convinced I became that the stories were real and I was right. Being right was extremely important to me. There was no doubt in my mind that I was right and those who harmed me were wrong in their treatment of me.

My self-talk had solidified those interpretations in my subconscious. From that point forward my *self-contrived stories* affected my relationship with my dad, my sister, my teachers and everyone else. I came to believe that no one loved me. More deeply, I believed it was true.

I hated my dad and my sister for not loving me. I became defensive and combative. As time passed, I assumed that I would never be liked or accepted by anyone, so why bother.

I wanted to be somebody. I wanted to be respected and to be right sometime, or at least not look too bad in the eyes of others. I had no idea it was the stories I had told myself over and over again and the feelings hidden deep inside my subconscious that kept me from looking good to anyone.

My perceptions and interpretations of what happened to me was not my dad's, my teacher's, or my sister's perceptions and interpretations. My perceptions and interpretations were my own. I had created those stories in my own mind. My father, sister and teachers had different perceptions and interpretations of those events. They have their own embellished stories to tell. You can imagine why we did not get along.

Looking back on childhood memories, and analyzing the image I had created for myself, I realize it was an image of failure in all areas of my life. The self-talk that I embellished and constantly repeated, even though I was not aware of doing so, had done its damage.

• • •

LACKING FOCUS

I remember lacking focus. I had the attention span of a gnat. Perhaps if I had been examined and diagnosed, I might have been labeled with Attention Deficit Disorder (ADD). The fact is, I had lost all sense of focus or a desire to achieve. I just didn't care!

My teachers saw me as defiantly lazy and inattentive. Lack of focus had made the learning process more difficult for me. I spent most of my time daydreaming and looking out classroom windows, a pastime my parents hoped I would outgrow. I still find myself staring out the window at times and, although it is not practical, I would prefer learning through osmosis.

My habit of not paying attention and always wanting to be right about everything led to many confrontations. It did not help build good relationships, especially with my teachers, parents, friends, and siblings. Many years later I learned that the subconscious absorbs everything and is capable of storing the most insignificant things, even when we are not conscious of it.

The information provided by my teachers that most all the students in my classes learned through attentive listening and participation went in one of my ears and out the other; however, I must have absorbed some of the information subliminally. After all, I did finally graduate.

My constant daydreaming caused my father to say derogatory things, which in my view demonstrated his feelings toward me and deepened my conviction that he did not love me.

When Dad and I were together, we argued about my dreams and personal habits. The conversation would usually end with his favorite line, "Talking to you is like talking to a brick wall. It is a total waste of time. If you don't pay attention and change your attitude, *you will never amount to a hill of beans.*"

Though my father may not have realized what he was doing at the time, he was challenging me. He was trying, as most parents do, to get his child to pay attention and to make better grades. It was important to him that I become an academic achiever so that I would have a better future than he had when he was growing up. At that time though, I believed he really meant the things he said, and his words hurt deeply. How I perceived and interpreted life's events put my mind in a stressful fog.

• • •

NOT QUALIFIED

When I entered the tenth grade my high school counselor advised me to forget college. "Unfortunately, you are not college material. Learning a trade of some sort would be a better way to spend you time while in school. You should consider Distributive Education (retail/service) or Cooperative Education (building trades)."

Telling me I was not college material was just another way of saying, "You are not qualified. You are a waste of time. *You will never amount to a hill of beans.*"

THE POWER OF SELF-IMAGING

Not that there is anything wrong with attending a trade school or working on a job where getting dirty is often required, it just wasn't what I had in mind. My dream was to own my own business, become rich and make my parents proud of me (a subconscious desire for praise and recognition). No doubt, I thought, that would blow their minds for sure, especially my father's.

Owning my own business became a goal that *I had to have*. By owning my own business I believed I would finally be somebody. The question remained: how could I achieve this goal while attending high school only half of the time?

My counselor believed my parents could not afford to send me to college. He believed I lacked the necessary academic requirements and skills to pass a college entrance exam. My academic history was there for him to see. He had my records. How could he be wrong?

I imagined my counselor thinking that even if my parents could afford to send me to college, few universities would have been interested in having a low academic achiever as one of their students.

My high school counselor was not the first to say, "You don't qualify". All my life the mental programming from those around me and from my own self-talk matched those words that kept ringing in my ears, "You don't qualify. You are nobody—an insignificant human being. *You will never amount to a hill of beans.*"

• • •

REVERSE PSYCHOLOGY
Reverse psychology does work occasionally, as it did for me.

Based on what? I thought. Not that I would compare myself to Albert Einstein, but he didn't pass his first college entrance exam either. So what? I rationalized. Who are *they* by whom I must measure myself?

What about Abraham Lincoln? He didn't have a formal education, and yet he became a lawyer, and after many failures running for public office, he eventually became President of the United States.

According to many books that have been written about Abraham Lincoln, he turned out being one of the greatest presidents who ever lived.

"What magic crystal ball do you have, Mr. Counselor, that could possibly give you enough information to judge another person?" I thought.

Realizing we were not wealthy, I was finally convinced there was no way to pursue a college education. With a bull-headed attitude, one of the traits I inherited from my father, I said to myself, "What makes you folks think you are so smart? You don't know me. I don't really know myself yet."

After feeling sorry for myself for a period of time and thinking through my choices, coupled with my strong desire to prove to everyone in the whole world that they were wrong about me, I set out on my life's journey.

The ball was in my court, so-to-speak. I realized at that moment that if I were going to reach my goals in life, it would be necessary to re-educate myself. I would need to change.

The counselor had angered me, my teachers angered me, my dad angered me, my sister angered me, and I thought, "You just hide in the bushes and watch!" I had to prove them wrong about me. I now had *reasons strong enough* to pursue my goals—goals *I had to achieve*. I was determined to follow my own dreams, not someone else's plans for me. I was determined to own my own business someday. With this clear goal in mind, my life began to change.

As a start, I finally listened and followed my counselor's advice and became a Distributive Education student, where I was first introduced to the retail business, an industry that I fell in love with.

I had no idea how I was going to achieve my dream of success, as I imagined success to be. I didn't have a dime, but I had determination and a *reason strong enough* to try. I was determined to prove to everyone that I could be more than a hill of beans. Surely the stories that I would be able to tell in the future would be stories of success, much wealth, and respect.

In retrospect, the many stories developed through my creative thinking were just that: thoughts in my head, self-talk, energy gone astray. It was self-talk that created the mental baggage and kept me from recognizing the true being that I am. That mental baggage kept me from having a loving relationship with my father on earth and my heavenly father.

It is the buried secrets, those false perceptions, self- imposed, embellished interpretations of life events that have destroyed more lives than all the wars ever fought.

4
Mental Baggage

Whatever we plant in our subconscious mind and nourish with repetition and emotion will one day become a reality.

—Earl Nightingale

RESEARCH INTO HOW the brain and mind works made me realize that the perception and interpretation of past events helped create my negative stories. I had unconsciously created the stories to justify my feelings about myself and about those around me, stories that made me believe I was right and they were wrong. The negative mental chatter had created all the challenges that seemed to surround me every day. I had loaded my mental baggage with so much negativity that it was weighing me down.

You will never amount to a hill of beans gave me a *reason strong enough* to motivate me to take action. Realizing that I would turn out being exactly what my negative thinking was dictating made me begin this process. For me, it was a major self-discovery.

We become what we think about. Thoughts become things. *Reasons strong enough* is what makes us move forward. This realization helped me evaluate the mental baggage I had carried around with me all my life.

Without *reasons strong enough* you might not discover the mental baggage that is holding you back. Wanting to change, hoping things will get better, will not make things better or change anything. If you have to change, if you have to get better, *if you have to have it*, and you have *reasons strong enough* to motivate you to action, you will surely reach your goals in life. To change, you must become a seeker. To become a seeker you have to have *reasons strong enough* to do the work of seeking.

During the process of self-imaging, you will come to realize that until you come to grips with the negative subconscious issues that possess you (mental baggage), you will have challenges discovering your preordained purpose in life.

As you continue your quest to discover *who you are, what you are*, and *why you are here*, you will discover that you have been and continue to be mentally programmed with negative mental baggage that no one would deliberately wish for.

Another discovery that will become apparent is that self-motivation, a conscious decision to take action toward a pre-determined goal *on your own*, without the prodding or supervision of others, is often stymied because of negative mental baggage piled high in your subconscious.

Mental baggage can come in many forms, all of which can take their toll on your ability to function in a positive way. Mental baggage affects your ability to form a positive self-image, and it will most definitely have a disabling effect on your self-esteem.

Mental baggage can come from child abuse, sexual abuse, mental and verbal abuse, rape, and many other traumatic events. It can be as simple as a constant flow of seemingly innocent negative put downs from friends, employers, co-workers, total strangers, and even close family members, as happened in my case.

Mental baggage can also come from events in your dreams or events that you have personally witnessed. It could be something that happened to characters in a movie or in a book, or traumatic events that happened to someone you know or have heard about. It could be traumatic events presented to you in such a realistic and emotional way that over time your subconscious accepts those events, not as something that happened to someone else, but as things that actually happened to you. It does not matter where the negative programming that creates the mental baggage comes from, it will do its damage regardless.

• • •

EGO

Sooner or later, in your quest to discover your whole self— *who you are, what you are, why you are here*—you will realize the voice in your head that you have been listening to most often is the voice of ego. Ego is the entity in your head that wants you to believe IT is the sum of all that you are. IT wants you to believe that the things you own, such as your home, the car you drive, your toys, your profession, the professional title you hold, and the reputation you have, are the things that measure you. Ego would have you believe these things represent who you are to the world. Ego does its work on the subconscious, where it feeds on things that falsely say, "This is who I am." We can recognize its voice and its sales pitch through the constant mental noise we call self-talk.

IT wants you to believe that if you don't have all the stuff that you are supposedly measured by...well, you just won't fit in and *you won't amount to a hill of beans*. You begin to believe deep inside that it must be true. You tend to do what Ego asked you to do all the while thinking that the voice you are hearing is your own.

You have a name that was given to you by your parents, but you are not your name. There are probably thousands of people in the world with a name exactly like yours. You may have a job, but you are not your job. Your career is something you have. It is not who you are.

THE POWER OF SELF-IMAGING

You may own a car, but you are not your car. The things you have are just personal assets. They are just things...your stuff. Things do not represent who you are, but Ego would have you believe otherwise. Ego would have you believe you are the reflection in the mirror.

Mental baggage is stored in the subconscious in many forms that appear real to us. Scientists dedicated to the study of the brain, mind, and human consciousness, point out that the subconscious mind does not know the difference between what is real and what is not. It does not know the difference between the truth and a lie. The subconscious mind does not care. Similar to the hard drive installed in computers, the subconscious mind is programmed—garbage in, garbage out.

Your combination of constant thinking (energy within the conscious mind), draws upon stored experiences within the subconscious mind, and instantaneously directs all your activity. Thus, what you perceive to be your reality in the current moment is created.

The subconscious mind is constantly receiving, sending, and storing sensory nerve impulses. The conscious mind searches for information stored in the subconscious, compares it to current conditions in context, and uses the data as needed. This amazing feat happens in nanoseconds.

• • •

SERVANT OF THE MIND
The brain is the servant of the mind. It is the mind that tells the brain to move your fingers while typing on the computer keyboard or playing an instrument. The brain acts on your mind's command, not the other way around.

Everything you experience is stored in your subconscious mind, and you are capable of recalling the smallest detail. It's all in there—the good, the bad and the ugly.

If you had to eat worms, but have never tasted a worm, would you know what a worm tastes like? You can only imagine; however, once you've eaten a worm, you will never forget the fact that you ate a worm or what it tastes like. You will no longer have to imagine. The memory of eating the worm and what it tastes like is permanently stored in your subconscious from that moment forward. Everything you have ever touched, smelled, tasted, heard, or seen is programmed and permanently stored away for recall.

It is your conscious mind that trains the neurons in your brain to remember. Conscious thoughts instruct the subconscious mind to find and use the exact position, movement and finger required to achieve its purpose when playing musical instruments. Repetition helps store the information in the subconscious for recall whenever it is needed. Once you've learned to ride a bike, drive a car, or even swing a golf club, you never forget how to do those things.

If you've never played the piano, could you play a simple tune like "Chop Sticks" without first mentally training your brain to direct your fingers to certain keys that create the musical notes? Look at it this way: the brain is hardware. The mind is energy. The brain is the servant of the mind. The thinking mind never stops.

Eckhart Tolle, author of *The Power of Now*, says, "The beginning of freedom is the realization that you are not the possessing entity—the thinker. Knowing this enables you to observe the entity. The moments you start watching the thinker, higher levels of consciousness become activated."

The good news is that you can release the mental baggage from your hard drive. Start listening! By listening I mean *being aware* of the voice in your head. When you begin to listen, you will have access to change.

• • •

DECOMPRESS AND FORGIVE
During this time, realize the need to bring your secrets to the forefront of your conscious mind and decompress them by convincing your subconscious mind that your stories are mostly false and extremely

exaggerated. You also need to forgive yourself for whatever it is that you believe you have done wrong and forgive those who you believe have wronged you. Realize that in ninety-nine percent of the cases, people who offended you would apologize if given a chance. Why hold it inside? Deal with it now.

5
Self-Talk

For as he thinketh in his heart, so is he.

—**Proverbs 23:7**

IT IS NOT only physical or mental abuse that causes a person's mental baggage and often a poor self-image; a poor self-image is more often caused by the way a person reacts to his experiences. What a person says to himself as he observes his world, and how he perceives and interprets those traumatic emotional experiences, does the most damage.

According to experts, we spend most of our time talking to ourselves. We spend a great deal of time talking to ourselves about our current problems, our past failures, and trying to find solutions.

Even in our sleep we are constantly hashing over the past, pondering what happened, what was said, who's at fault, who is right, and who is wrong. We also spend a great deal of time talking to ourselves about the future, considering what is going to happen, and what we wish would happen. We talk to ourselves about our hopes and dreams. We talk to ourselves constantly, and it is the things we say to ourselves that direct our actions. It's the things we say to ourselves

THE POWER OF SELF-IMAGING

that make us believe we are who we say we are. All this self-talk gets imbedded in our subconscious mind.

If you don't want a particular thing in your life, don't say it mentally or orally. Be aware of your thoughts. Notice what you are saying to yourself. The words mentally spoken in silence and aloud become things.

Thoughts of the mind instruct the subconscious mind. The subconscious does not care if it is true or false. It begins to act on the mental command based on your belief system. What you think about, what you say to yourself, becomes your reality.

Joseph Murphy, Ph.D., D.D., author of *The Power of Your Subconscious Mind*, says:

> The captain is the master of his ship, and his decrees are carried out. In the same way, your conscious mind is the captain and the master of your ship—your body, your environment, and all your affairs. Your subconscious mind takes the orders you give it, based upon what your conscious mind believes and accepts as the truth. It does not question the orders or the basis on which they are given.
>
> If you repeatedly say to yourself, "I can't afford it," your subconscious mind takes you at your word. It sees to it that you will not be in a position to buy what you want. As long as you go on saying, "I can't afford that car, that vacation, that home," you can be sure your subconscious mind will follow your orders. You will go through life experiencing the lack of all these things, and you will believe that circumstances made it so. It will not occur to you that you have created those circumstances yourself, by your own negative, denying thoughts.

What we say to ourselves forms the direction for our life. Negative self-talk can lead to devastating illness, including mental depression, even suicide. Negative self-talk is an instigator. It is the major cause of mental baggage.

Julie K. Hersh, in her book *Struck by Living, From Depression to Hope*, describes the thoughts of her mind during a traumatic period in her life:

> After leaving the business world to care for small children and aging grandparents, as well as adapting to a culture far different from that of my upbringing, I evaporated into my surroundings, no longer sure of who I was. What was my purpose? What did I want? These questions cratered me, setting in motion my genetic tendency for depression. Most people answer these questions without a tour of the psychiatric ward, but my road was bumpy—the psych ward was only one of many stops.
>
> I tried to kill myself three times.

Julie now travels extensively speaking to large and small audiences, wherever she can find them, about her self-imposed thoughts and genetic tendency toward depression that led to thoughts of suicide. She does this in hopes that she will be able to reach others before they sink into a state of mind that could end in death.

The orders you give to your subconscious mind based on what you believe to be true about your past and present circumstances will be carried out. It does not care whether the orders are good or bad, true or false. It simply follows the directions given. One should pay close attention to this fact.

In the process of improving your self-image, you will learn to fight fire with fire. You will give instructions to your engine room through self-talk, the very thing that caused your problem to begin with. You will claim I AM positive statements of faith as fact, even though in the present moment the perceived facts may not coincide with what you really believe to be true.

I AM affirmations can help overcome self-deceit, clean the mind of mental garbage and open the door to finding your true self, the person you really are.

6
Beginning the Process

We achieve inner health only through forgiveness—the forgiveness not only of ourselves, but others.

—Joshua Loth Leibman

REPROGRAMMING YOUR SUBCONSCIOUS mind's conceptual view of the person you believe you are, your self-image, is a process. It requires excepting as fact things that you may not yet understand.

Regardless of your prior mental programming, when you develop a more positive mental picture of the person you really are, you will move to more exciting possibilities. You will be enabled to discover your life's purpose that has been eluding you.

The process of self-imaging is not a quick fix. It will require your steadfast commitment to personal change. Otherwise, going through this process will be a waste of your time.

The fact that you have committed to reading this book is a positive indicator that you are serious about making changes in your life. If you choose to proceed, what you should hope to accomplish is self-awareness in its truest form.

It is difficult to become aware of your true self while being controlled by your ego. Ego works hard to force you to justify your thinking in the way it would have you believe. It will try to convince you it is right in all its assumptions about the person you have turned out being. Ego will continue its relentless effort to convince you that you are who and what it says you are.

In order to continue to justify its position of "being right" in how you turned out being, ego will try to convince you that the false stories you tell yourself and others about who you are, are true. Ego is the entity that speaks loudly in your head. LISTEN TO ME! YOU ARE WHO I SAY YOU ARE.

Ego does not want to hear about your desire to change, to improve or to be more than it says you are. Ego will tell you, you do not need to change. You are already all you will ever be. You are already better than anyone else. However, you should understand that consistent awareness of ego eliminates ego's ability to function. You can change!

• • •

MAKING THIS WORK FOR YOU

In order to make this process work for you, it will be necessary to realize that ego is not your soul, the 'spirit-self,' as some would have you believe. Ego is a controlling entity inside you that wants to dominate your thoughts. Ego wants you to believe you are slightly better than anyone else. In order to make this process work for you, it will be necessary to become acutely aware of the voice of ego.

In order to make this process work for you, it will also be necessary to enter into a period of forgiveness. Forgiving yourself and others who have been involved in traumatic events that have occurred in your life is essential. Once you have uncovered the truth ego has so carefully concealed, new opportunities will open up for you. Fantastic possibilities that you have not previously realized will introduce themselves to you. Your ego, however, will try to convince you that it is not your place to forgive anyone, especially yourself. It will tell you that you are right in your assumptions about the person you already are. Ego will tell you that the stories you have told yourself are true, so why deny their existence or content?

You can never fully destroy ego. It is always there, lurking in the shadows of your mind, pushing you, prodding, and trying to take control. Be aware of ego!

• • •

WANTING, NEEDING AND HAVING
You should be cognizant that change begins with the realization that there is a huge difference in *wanting* something, *needing* something, and *having to have* something. Even though you might think you need to make changes in your life in order to have more things; more travel, more friends, more money, it does not necessarily mean that you are serious or that you *have to have* it.

You might want to go to Italy, but don't necessarily have to; therefore, the trip to Italy will just remain one of the things to do when the time comes…maybe. However, if it becomes a burning desire and you have to go to Italy, you *have to have it*, then you will find a way to go to Italy.

Wherever it is that you have to go, or whatever it is you *have to have*, or you *have to do,* you will achieve. If you don't *have to have it*, you probably won't. If you believe you *have to have* changes occur in your life, then you are on the right path to a fantastic future.

Think for a moment! You most likely already have everything that you really need to survive, things that you *have to have*: a roof over your head, food, a bed, clothes, access to healthcare, companionship, love. What else, then, do you *have to have*? Could it be a sense of knowing who you really are that haunts you? Could it be a feeling of emptiness, the feeling that something is missing, that you are not really complete as a person? What is it that you really *have to have* to fill that hole in your life? Affirm the things that you *have to have* in your life and that void will be filled abundantly.

An affirmation is affirming a thing as though it is already so. An affirmation can be the fire in your gut that burns the negative thoughts. Affirmations can be the wall between you and those who say you can't. An affirmation says I AM.

• • •

HOW TO CREATE AN AFFIRMATION

Creating affirmations based on what you *have to have* in your life is important to making this process work. In order for this process to work for you, you must first begin with changing the mental forces that have caused you to believe that *you will never amount to a hill of beans*. Curing the *I can't disease* is done through positive statements of faith.

To continue the process of self-imaging, make a list of the things you *have to have*.

For some, this task is very difficult because they have been so beaten up by negative events and negative self-talk that they find it very difficult to make such a list. The very idea that they can be more than they have turned out being is often extremely difficult to believe.

When asked to make of list of things they *have to have*, a bucket list of sorts, people often tell me, "I don't know what I really *have to have*. A million dollars, a big house a Rolls Royce, my own private airplane, and world travel…I don't know. There are lots of things I would like to have, but I am never going to have those things. I would just be kidding myself to list those things."

My response is that you don't know what is possible. True, those things are just material things. It is stuff that your self-talk has told you that you don't deserve because you are a nobody, a person *that will never amount to a hill of beans*. But, the truth is, you can have all those things and more if you really *have to have* them. Quiet often,

THE POWER OF SELF-IMAGING

when things are at their darkest point in our life, out of desperation you take action, when otherwise, we would not. Believing we cannot, while onsumed with the I can't disease. You will always get what you *have to have*. You are preordained to succeed. Why not try?

• • •

DESPERATION

Let's imagine if you will, that you have a young daughter that has a very rare, incurable illness that can lead to death very quickly if not treated at a prescribed time with a very expensive drug. In fact, if your child does not take the prescribed pill in the prescribed time, she could die within hours.

Let's also imagine that it is two o'clock in the morning on a Sunday when your daughter awakens crying. You must give her the pill, but you discover you are out of the pills. Somehow, you forgot to refill the prescription the prior day. What would you do? Would you get her pills for her?

Silly question isn't it! Of course, you would get the pills for her. Surely, you would do what ever you had to do to get her medicine, even if you had to break into the drug store to do it. Nothing would stop you. You would get what you *have to have*.

If you don't have to change, if you don't need to improve, if you don't care who you are, what you are or why you are here, you will never know. On the other hand, if you have to change, if you have to change now, you will do what you have to do to make that happen. You always get what you *have to have*.

The first step to getting what you *have to have* is to affirm it as fact, not as something you wish you had, but as something you already have. In fact, if you really think about it, you already have everything you believe you *have to have* at this point in time.

Once you've made your list of things you *have to have*, write an "I am statement of faith" (affirmation) for each item on your list. Place each affirmation on a separate piece of paper or on 4 X 6 card.

Write the affirmation as though you already possess the item or goal you've set for yourself. Have faith! Do not be concerned with the time it takes to complete this process.

Forget about the money. As motivation speaker Jim Rohn says, "Success is looking for someone to land on." Money will always follow success. Money will come, but first you have to have a big dream. If you *have to have* it, you will get it.

Paint a complete picture. What? How big? What color? How much? How many? Describe that perfect job. What you will do, what you are willing to sacrifice to obtain it, how much money you expect to earn, etc.

Cut out pictures of the things you *have to have* and the places you have to go to. Place them on your refrigerator, or build a dream board and place it where you will see it several times a day. Your dream board will help you visualize what you *have to have*. Remember, what the mind can conceive and believe it can achieve.

More important, in addition to tangible goals, write affirmations that deal with intangible goals, such as self-improvement, family relationships, and personal changes you have to make in your own life. Describe the person you want to turn out being. What would you want written on your tombstone? What would you want your friends and family to say about you when it's over? Begin each affirmation with *I AM*, the two most powerful words in any language.

Once your affirmations are written, commit to them. Read one affirmation at a time for thirty days, four times each day. Read your affirmation upon waking, before lunch, once before dinner, and aloud at bedtime. After thirty days, put the affirmation in a shoebox and store it away. Then begin the second affirmation and so forth.

Keep your dream board alive. Add new items when you feel you *have to have* something. Rejoice and celebrate your successes, but never forget to be grateful.

You can have anything you *have to have*, but you must remember that things are only loaned to you. In the truest sense, you can possess things, but you cannot really own anything. In the end you cannot take your possessions with you. As you progress you will be astonished to realize how much you have achieved and how much you have personally changed.

As you read the affirmations at the end of the following chapters, be intensely aware of the change in your personal attitude and how you feel about yourself. In addition, before announcing to your family and friends that you are involved in this process, prove to yourself that this process will work for you.

Friends and family, who do not understand the process of self-imaging, along with those who have not read this book, may try to discourage you. They will try to steal your dream. Remember that it is your personal desire for change, not theirs. As you progress and begin to see changes in your own life, notice how your friends and family's attitude towards you begin to change. Notice how their attitude seems to be more positive and supportive of you.

Hold on to the dreams in your heart,
Never allow them to die,
Life's snowy storms will depart,
And in the winds of trial you'll find space to try.

Hold on to the dreams in your heart,
Never let them stray,
Even when you don't know how to start,
Somehow you'll find the way.

—Joel D. Johnson

Affirmation 1
I am clearing from my subconscious mind the cobwebs of ill conceived, poorly perceived, and fallaciously interpreted, self-imposed stories that for too long have forced me to suffer a life of self-deceit.

I am reborn into a life filled with love, happiness, and abundance.

I am grateful to the Spirit of the Universe for making me unique among all creatures in the entire universe. There is no one exactly like me and there will never be another person exactly like me.

I am thankful to the Spirit of the Universe for abiding in me and for giving me the wisdom to know that, though I am not complete, I am at this moment in time and space the person I am meant to be.

Today I am being molded as a potter molds a uniquely beautiful vase. I cannot fail. All things are possible through the Spirit of the Universe that lives in me.

7
Secrets of the Heart

The only thing that stands between a man and what he wants from life is often merely the will to try it and the faith to believe that it is possible.

—**Richard M. DeVos**

BECOMING AND BEING overshadow and consume the thinking mind. We are so busy doing this and that, and being what ego says we should be that we become consumed with the *being* and *doing* and miss the moment, where all of life experiences occur. In the process we forget what life is really about.

Ego would have us believe that if we stay busy doing and becoming what it says we should be doing and becoming, the anger and guilt caused by the secrets of the heart, the mental baggage, secrets in the mental closet, or whatever you choose to call them, will somehow subside or go away. Ego would have you believe that all the *doing* and *becoming* will fill the unfulfilled emptiness inside. If this is true, then I must ask, how is that working for you?

Secrets of the heart reflect on your face and in your eyes. You may try to hide your facial expressions and body language that show your innermost thoughts and feelings, but if a person looks closely enough into your eyes, he or she will find your truth there. Even with extensive training, it is extremely hard for you to hide the thoughts and emotions that are naturally expressed in body language and facial expressions.

The fear of trying, the fear of failure, and yes, even the fear of success, show in your facial expression when you are asked, "Why not you? Why not try? Why not now? If not now, when? If not you, who?" The voice may answer firmly, but the eyes give away your true feelings.

The self-defeating negative self-talk repeated over and over again in your head and shared with others in conversation causes you to feel inadequate and directs your actions away from your desired goals.

A person with a poor self-image will be filled with poor self-esteem, the feeling that, "I am no good." You may not be aware of it, but you will get the very thing you do not want when you say, "I'm not good enough!" "I'm too fat!" "I'm too skinny!" "No one loves me!" "No one really cares whether I live or die!" "I'm not smart enough!" "What do they expect?" "I'm not perfect you know!" "I can't do it!" "I can't afford it!" "I just don't have what it takes to succeed!" "I will always be a follower." "I am just not cut out to be a leader." "I'll never amount to a hill of beans." Are these the things you want in your life? Is this how you want to turn out being? Is this how you want to feel about yourself? If not, don't say it. Don't think it!

• • •

CHANGE REQUIRES INTEGRITY

In order to change, you must have integrity. What is integrity? Integrity means being truthful with yourself and the world. It means you will keep your word. Integrity means whatever you say you will do in your affirmations or promises made, you will do and you will do it when promised. Whenever you give your word you are saying, "My word is my bond. You can count on it. What ever I say I will do, I will do."

Most people want to be honest with themselves and to those with whom they associate. Most people want to feel good about the person they have become, and they want to look good to the world. In fact, looking good is so important to some people that they will promise anything. It is so important to some people that they will try to cover mistakes with lies, hoping their lies will never be discovered. Can you believe that? People who do this lack integrity. To make real change work for you, real integrity is vital.

When you promise to make the changes that you *have to have*, even though it does not seem possible, you are promising yourself that you will keep your word. You will keep your word even while you are hearing voices in your head that tell you that you are wasting your time.

You promise to keep your word when you say to yourself that you will expose the secrets held hostage in your subconscious. What secrets? They are secrets of the heart, blown out of such proportion that they could become a best selling future box office movie; secrets, if written in a book might become a number one best seller on the New York Times Best Seller List; secrets you plan to tell someone, maybe even to the world someday. Meanwhile, secrets of the heart will continue to camouflage the real person that you are, but by being a person of integrity, you will do what you promise yourself. You will do what it takes to change. When the negativism associated with these secrets is released, you will be free to move on with your life.

Some people, subconsciously, want to hang on to their negative baggage, if you can believe that. If they dispose of these mind-boggling secrets, who then will they be? Will the bucket then be empty? If they admit to that one-night-stand, the abortion, lies told, hearts broken and broken promises, will I be harshly judged? They wonder. Will they lose it all? What then?

If you are truthful with yourself, you will agree that the only way to free yourself from this agonizing mental baggage is to expose it and deal with it right now. If you found a poisonous snake in your bed, would you sleep with it? How soon would you put distance between you and it? How soon would you get rid of it? Tomorrow? How do you think you will feel when the snake is dead?

If you had to write down all your personal secrets of the heart in a spiral notebook, which by now have become "my story", and were required to hold the notebook extended straight out to the side, as though handing the book to someone, after a while the notebook would get heavier and heavier. Soon the weight would be so unbearable that you could no longer hold your arm up. The burden of holding your secrets of the heart would be more than you could take. Regardless, there will come a time when you must let go of the notebook and when you do, you will be extremely relieved and happy that it is finally exposed.

Most people, however, will continue to assume that by exposing their hidden secrets it will make them look bad to the world. The pain of not looking good to the world or to themselves is often more than they can bear. Some people would rather sleep with a snake. Exposing the secrets hidden in their mental closet will not be easy, but people can change if they have the integrity to be honest with themselves and the world.

If you are serious about changing your future to a life filled with happiness and true self-awareness, the first thing you need to do is forgive yourself and then forgive those you have harmed and those you believe have harmed you. Once you have truly forgiven yourself and those who have harmed you, go back in your mind to the event where you felt violated. Picture the event in your mind, not according to the story you now tell yourself, but the bare bone truth of what happened. If possible, visit the people involved by phone or in person and ask them to share with you their perception of the event and how they perceived and are interpreting the event today. You might be astonished that the stories you have been telling yourself do not match their reality at all.

As an example: The following story I had kept buried in my mind all my life. When going through the process of exposing my own secrets

THE POWER OF SELF-IMAGING

to the world, I confronted my oldest sister, Shirley, to see what her perception and interpretation was of the following events.

When I was about one and half years old, my mother put me in a cardboard box at the end of a cotton row in the cotton patch and asked Shirley to watch me.

Mother was picking cotton and my sister was playing in the sand a few feet away. Somehow, the box had been placed on top of an anthill, the home of some very large red ants. Before long I was covered with these red ants who became angry about having their entrance blocked, and I was stung many times. I screamed and cried until it drove everyone nearly crazy. Shirley was not concerned.

Mother, hearing me cry, came to see what was wrong and found me covered with the ants. She grabbed me from the box, dusted the ants off and tried to console me until I calmed down a bit. My mother accused my sister of not watching me, and punished her.

The truth was, I was one and half years old and my sister was four. What did she know? She did not set me down on the anthill; mother must have, without realizing it.

What did I know? In fact, the only way I could have known about that event was if someone told me about it after I was much older. As the story was told to me, long since forgotten, they accused my sister of deliberately setting the box down on the anthill. "Shirley probably set you in that box on top of the anthill on purpose so she would not have to watch you again." This was said in jest, of course. None-the-less, that story told to me by someone in the family many years ago remained a secret in my mental closet. It became part of my mental baggage. Although the story was not deliberately distorted, over the years it caused me to distant myself from my wonderful sister.

When I confronted my sister about this event several years ago, she said she would never have put that box with me in it on top of an anthill. She said, "In the first place, I was only four. I could not have picked you up in that box and carried you to a mound of ants. Where did you get such a crazy story?" She did, however, remember getting punished for all those ants biting me, but said she was innocent and that mom was just striking out in anger, not realizing that she was probably the guilty one.

You can't change the past, but you can forgive and ask for forgiveness. I can laugh about that event now, since we know the truth.

How strange! It never dawned on me that she could not have picked that box up with me in it. This goes to show how the mind works. My self-talk about that event and others shaped my feelings toward my sister and myself.

• • •

AFFIRMING THE DESIRES OF YOUR HEART
Words are powerful. What you say to yourself has shaped the person you are. Self-talk is the reason you have turned out being the person you are at this moment in time.

Negative and positive thoughts become pictures in your mind that are automatically stored in your subconscious. These autosuggestions you have affirmed have dictated your memories of the past, control your present moment, and determine your imagined future.

The dictionary says an *affirmation is the assertion that something exists or is true, as in affirming a fact as if it were so.* Creating positive affirmations help make change possible.

Affirmations are similar to prayers. Prayers work best when you don't doubt the outcome. It means you have faith that the outcome will be positive. To pray for something, and not believe the prayer will be answered, is a waste of breath.

Jesus said, while healing the blind man, "Your faith has healed you." If the blind man did not believe, if he did not have faith, would he have asked to be healed? Did he believe he would be healed if Jesus touched him? Absolutely! How did he know that? The blind man affirmed that. He probably said to himself, when Jesus touches me, I will be healed. He believed it and he acted on it.

Affirmations are much like self-induced hypnotic suggestion. They work in the subconscious through personal faith that the affirmation will deliver the desired result. Affirmations alone have no power until one decides to take the necessary steps to fulfill the desire. The blind man took the necessary steps in faith. He reached out and asked in faith.

Affirmation without action may lead to depression, anxiety and stress. Affirmations without action are only wishful thinking. Let's get started.

Do not begin affirmation number two until you have read affirmation number one for thirty days.

Affirmation 2

I am a new person. I face the world with a new attitude and with complete confidence and belief that persistent efforts toward my preordained purpose will bring me the personal changes and rewards I seek.

I am not concerned with time for time is only an illusion.

On any difficult journey I know that in order for me to reach my final destination, I must believe I can; I must know I can; I must have faith that I can. Otherwise, why should I bother to attempt a hike to the top of a mountain, where the path is unknown to me?

I am persisting in faith and I will continue until I reach the top of my mountain. I cannot fail.

8
Faith to Believe

Faith is to believe what we do not see, and the reward of this faith is to see what we believe.

—St. Augustine

IN ORDER TO expose the secrets hidden away in your subconscious mind and make the changes in your life that you so strongly desire, you must have faith and confidence in your ability to climb that mountain.

For an affirmation to work for you, you must first have faith that it is possible, even though your current belief and understanding about your own personal abilities may not coincide with the words that you affirm. If you stop to think about it for a moment, you will have to agree that most people have a tendency to have faith in things and in people they don't even know.

When we travel by air we have faith the plane is in good working order and that the pilot knows his job well enough to fly it. We have faith the plane will arrive at its destination safely or we would not get on it in the first place.

When we buy a car we have faith that our new car is manufactured properly and will not disassemble while we are traveling down the highway at seventy miles per hour, often only minutes after driving off the dealer's lot.

In other situations we have faith the elevator we ride will not take a sudden free fall; faith the medicine the doctor prescribes for us will cure us and not cause us to become addicted or kill us; faith the drill our dentist uses won't suddenly slip and cause him to do a frontal lobotomy; faith we will awaken after a night of wonderful sleep; faith our spouses will be faithful to us. We have faith in other people and in machines, yet often we do not have faith in ourselves.

Most people have been programmed to believe that if they pursue the right education, get the right breaks, and develop the necessary talent, they will have a good chance to succeed. They spend thousands of dollars, often going deep into debt, to obtain an education all because they believe and have faith that this is the formula that works best.

Unfortunately, the world is full of highly educated people who have been exposed to the right environment and who have great talent, yet still lack the success these things were supposed to bring. While education, talent and breaks are important, it is most often negative self-talk and lack of faith in their own abilities that keeps people from achieving their goals. Higher education is not to blame. It is most likely the voice in the head that keeps saying, "I can't" that keeps people from trying. Additionally, it is often the mental thought that says, "You will never amount to anything" that destroys their confidence and makes it hard to achieve their intended goal.

Mankind has gained more knowledge in the past one hundred years than has been accumulated in all of history. With each new discovery our knowledge multiplies and feeds on itself; yet, with all that knowledge, we still allow ourselves to be programmed with the idea that *we won't amount to a hill of beans.*

There are hundreds of schools and lots of people who are willing to help. Ask! If you believe, if you have faith, if you try, you can be anything you want to be. You can achieve all the things you want to achieve and more, *if you have to have it*. It is simply up to you.

> *It's a very funny thing about life; if you refuse to accept anything but the best, you very often get it.*
>
> —W. Somerset Maugham

• • •

THE I CAN'T DISEASE

Often, people contend that they don't have enough money or time to pursue their dreams, but time and money is no excuse. If you develop your idea, have faith it will work, and if you bring value to the marketplace, there will be lots of people willing to hand over their money.

Motivational speaker Jim Rohn says, "The world will stand aside and give up its capital to those who really believe in themselves and their dreams."

There are too many true 'rags to riches' stories to swallow the "I can't get the money" excuse. You can get the money. But first you have to get rid of the "I can't disease." You have to let go of the voice in your head that says, "I can't."

It is certainly not lack of time that keeps people from achieving. Currently, most people have more discretionary time at their disposal than any other period in recorded history. We always make the time we need to do the important things in our life when *we have to do it*. We always get what we want when we *have to have it*. Everyone has the same twenty-four hours each day. No one has more or less time than another person. Often the difference in becoming unbelievably wealthy and living a mediocre life style is making use of your non-productive time to develop the ideas and life style that you *have to have*. What are you doing with your non-productive time?

Don't let time be your crutch. Turn off the television, put down that novel, and turn that non-productive space into educating yourself. Start today doing the things you don't want to do in order to live a life most people could never dream possible. Start listening to the voice of possibilities. Your success is on the inside. Look there first.

Why not enjoy world travel and living in luxury? Others are enjoying true happiness, love, and a luxurious life style. Why not you? If not you…who? If not now…when? Have faith! You can do it! Life is short! Start now!

You have the power to change your negative subconscious programming by utilizing the very thing that created the picture you hold of yourself in the first place—self-talk. The never-ending voice in the head is merely mental chatter. It is through positive self-talk that you begin to edit your mental movie and begin the journey of using the real talents and abilities that have been provided to you as a gift. By acting on faith and by accepting the fact that you are already equipped and are ready to achieve great things, you will begin to visualize the many possibilities that await you. Your preordained purpose was installed in your brain at birth. It only awaits action. You cannot fail.

When you replace the false stories that you've kept hidden in the back of your mental closet with positive statement's of faith, those false stories will be recognized for what they are—myths. By confronting those false issues, you open the opportunity for change in your life.

By faithfully repeating your affirmations and believing the positive words, you will cause the subconscious to take *automatic action* in the direction of your life goals.

John says, "I get it now. All I have to do is decide what I want and repeat my 'I am statements of faith' and presto, I will get what I want. No problem!"

So John makes his list and creates his affirmation. "I am successful in all I do. I am earning $25,000 per month. Everyone loves me."

As he creates his affirmation, he is laughing to himself. Right away his subconscious mind, infected with the, I *can't disease*, steps in and answers his affirmation with its negative narration that is based on his past mental programming.

"Successful? Ha!" His subconscious says. "You can't even spell the word, much less be successful. And you can forget the $25,000 thing. You have to reach some level of success to earn that much income in one month, and you will never earn that much because you have never been successful at anything in your life. Besides, what could you possibly do to earn that much money every month?"

"Look, I have news for you—what makes you think everyone loves you? Your dad left when you were a year old and your mom gave you up for adoption when you were two. Your parents didn't love you. Where do you come up with all this stuff...it's just not true. Why can't you be honest with yourself?"

And so it goes every time he reads his affirmations, without realizing his negative thoughts are negating the things he wants in his life.

Keep in mind that you tend to take action on your most dominant thought, be it positive or negative. Thoughts create action and action creates things. Thoughts create the results in your life.

• • •

AFFIRMATION – BELIEF - FAITH – ACTION
It is important to remember that you must have faith, knowing that over time the words you repeat to yourself will bring forth the actions required to achieve the results you seek. You must believe the affirmations you repeat to yourself four times a day and you must have faith that by doing so the affirmations will bring to you the success and happiness you desire. Otherwise, why waste your time reading them?

In the process of repeating your affirmations, you will be editing your life movie titled "My Story" by clipping the false programming from your mental film. You must clip that data and place it in the wastebasket of your subconscious, replacing it with new thoughts, which will uplift, inspire, and move you to positive action.

Deepak Chopra, MD, in his book, *Ageless Body, Timeless Mind*, says, "Interpretations arise from a person's self-interaction. You experience this as internal dialogue. Thoughts, judgments, and feelings are ceaselessly swirling through one's mind: 'I like this, I don't like that, I'm afraid of A, I'm not sure of B, etc.' Internal dialogue is not random mental noise; it is generated from a deep level by your beliefs and assumptions."

In the *Holy Bible*, Matthew 17:20, Jesus replies to his disciples, when they asked why they could not wilt the fig tree, "Because of your unbelief: for verily I say unto you, if ye have faith as a grain of mustard seed, ye shall say unto this mountain, remove hence to yonder place; and it shall remove; and nothing shall be impossible unto you."

The process of self-imaging is not voodoo, nor is it a magic formula written on clay tablets discovered in a cave, nor handed down by an ancient soothsayer, nor some spiritual teacher living on top of the highest mountain somewhere; although that might make the contents of this book more interesting. The process of self-imaging is a process of self-discovery. It is about discovering the real truth about the person you believe you are and releasing the secrets of the heart from its bondage.

You must believe, you must have *faith* that at this point in time and space, you *are* the preordained person you are meant to be. While you may not understand, and you may find it difficult to accept, the things you *have to have* to live out your preordained purpose were chosen for you by the Spirit of the Universe. You are a spirit being, one with the Spirit of the Universe, filled with power to achieve His purpose for your life. It is why you are here. It is your destiny. You will not experience physical death until your preordained purpose has been achieved.

Affirmation 3
I am armed with faith, knowing and believing the Spirit of the Universe lives in me and directs my actions in mysterious ways. Though I am tested, I cannot fail.

I am mentally strong. I know that although I may face demons and other obstacles yet unknown, I will persist, knowing that nothing can keep me from achieving my preordained purpose. I cannot fail.

I am armed with faith, knowing all things are possible through the Spirit of the Universe that lives in me. I cannot fail.

9
Mental Hard Drive

The subconscious believes you have to have what the mind dwells on; therefore, you will receive what you think about.

—Joel Johnson

ALL THINGS ARE created and energized by the power of the Spirit of the Universe, and therefore belong to the Spirit of the Universe. Though ego would beg to differ, you cannot own anything.

Eckhart Tolle, author of *A New Earth*, says, "The ego identifies with having, but its satisfaction in having is relatively shallow and short-lived one. Concealed within it remains a deep-seated sense of dissatisfaction, of incompleteness, of "not enough." "I don't have enough yet," by which the ego really means, "I am not enough yet."

The things that are necessary for your physical survival are loaned to you. You can have anything you want, if you *have to have* it. One needs only to tap into the mental hard drive to access them. Unfortunately, if you dwell on things you do not want in your life, you often get that which you do not want as well.

THE POWER OF SELF-IMAGING 53

Everyone wants to be loved and appreciated, but if you are constantly saying to yourself, "I am no good," "No one loves me," "I can't do that," "I'll *never amount to a hill of beans*," "No one cares whether I live or die," and you believe that to be true, you are bringing forth the manifestation of those thoughts. What do you expect?

Your subconscious can easily be confused by the voice it hears in your head. Is it the good voice or the evil voice you hear, or is it the negative voice talking, or is it the self-centered ego telling you what to do? Your subconscious does not care from whom it takes its orders. It just does what it is told. The subconscious believes you *have to have* what the mind dwells on; therefore, you will receive what you ask for.

The conversations some people have with themselves are often filled with harsh words and self-degradation, which is enough to cause a lifetime of mental damage.

As a small boy I dwelled on the negative and I got what I asked for.

• • •

KICKING SAND
Most summers I looked forward to spending a few weeks with my grandparents on their vegetable farm just outside of Teaselville, Texas. It was my birthplace and the place I remember fondly as I grew up. I loved my grandparents and I loved spending time at their farm. After moving to the city, I could hardly wait to visit the farm each summer.

It was a beautiful warm summer evening. I should have been exhausted. We had worked in the cotton field chopping cotton all day. After supper, I decided to sneak away to my first cousin's house, which was a few hundred yards east, down the old sandy road. My uncle was not happy that I had come to visit so late in the day and refused to allow me to talk to Tootles.

As an adult looking back on this event, I now realize he was concerned with my safety and was not happy that I was walking that lonely stretch of road just before sundown. It was not unusual to find copperheads and rattlesnakes searching for food in the wild berry patches that grew next to the fence line alongside the road. What if I had decided to pick a few berries? With bare feet and my hands in the berry vines, anything could have happened to me. There were other wild animals that I should have been concerned with too, but at the time my only thought was visiting my cousin.

"GO HOME BOY!" he yelled. "It's too late for you to be running this country road. Now GIT back home." He almost tore the screen door off its hinges as he slammed the door in my face. I was shocked! His response was totally unexpected and out of character for him.

I slowly walked back up the sandy road to my grandparent's home. Hurt and embarrassed, I felt rejected and unloved. With tear-filled eyes that blurred my vision, head down and hands deep in the pockets of my stripped overalls, I angrily kicked the sand into the air. I wondered what was wrong with me. My ten-year-old mind felt foggy and incomplete. I wondered if I was missing a portion of my brain. It disturbed me that everyone else was so much smarter. I felt extremely ignorant.

"What is wrong with me?" I asked myself. Without realizing it, every word I spoke to myself was bringing me the very things I did not want in my life. Through my own self-criticism, I was programming my subconscious mind to believe I was ignorant, that something was wrong with my brain, and that no one loved me.

Uncle Robert had never treated me like that before. I was shocked. I felt unwanted and out of place. At that moment I believed Uncle Robert never really liked me and did not want me to visit cousin Glenda or anyone else in his family. My interpretation: Uncle Robert does not love me. No one loves me!

Swearing to myself never to return to his home again, while wiping away my tears, his words rattled my mind. I thought, "It would be a long time before Uncle Robert sees me again." And, for a very long time I refused to go to his home. I avoided him like a plague. This event separated he and my cousin Tootles, for a long time.

I have no idea what was going on in that house on that evening, but I had made the choice to go there. As it turned out, it was not a good choice.

THE POWER OF SELF-IMAGING

This sort of thing happened to me often. It seemed as though I was always in the way, always saying the wrong thing, getting yelled at for what I thought was for no apparent reason, and always making the wrong choices.

When someone asked me to do something, I was always eager to please, but sometimes I goofed up. I would often get distracted and get involved in something else and forget to do what I was asked to do. I would eventually get chewed out for it. I truly believed something was wrong with me. My self-talk confirmed that something was wrong with me, over and over again.

"Why can't I be smart like my big sister, like my cousins, like anybody? Why am I always letting people down, seldom pleasing them? Why can't people be nice to me?" I wondered. My thoughts were filled with negative self-talk and feelings of being unimportant, a no-body. I often wished that I had never been born.

I was not the perfect child. I was a little slow catching on to things, a big daydreamer, and a little on the lazy side as well, I was told. I was angry that I lacked the intelligence to understand things properly. I believed my teachers did not like me and were deliberately singling me out, and picking on me by asking such hard questions.

I had a tendency to ask too many questions, and when given the answer, I often argued about the answers out of frustration. I did not understand. Most of the time I had no facts on which to base my arguments. I thought arguing made me appear to be more interested and somewhat knowledgeable about the subject.

Recognizing that I was not paying attention, the teacher asked, "Joel, how much is three plus four?" Of course, as usual, I was daydreaming and had not been listening. I had been looking out the window and my mind was miles away.

"Six!" I answered quickly, partially stunned, and embarrassed that I was caught not paying attention. I heard giggles from my classmates. Right away I knew I had given the wrong answer.

"Didn't you do your homework?" She asked, with a disgusted look on her face. "The answer is seven!"

"How do you know that? Who made up all those numbers anyway?" I said, trying to save face.

"Joel, we will discuss this after class," she said as she moved on with the lesson by placing her attention on another student. None-to-soon for me! I knew I was in for a long day.

The fact is I had not cracked a book. I was so far behind the other students, I felt I would never catch up. "What's the use?" I thought.

I knew I was ignorant because people were constantly telling me so. Not in those words, but the inference was the same. I would put those folks down as often as I could. It made me feel satisfied that I was getting back at them for putting me down. Who were they to treat me in such a horrible way? I wished bad things would happen to them. I believed they deserved it and I looked forward to the day that they would get their due for treating me that way. I wanted to be there when it happened and yell out, "YOU HAD IT COMING!"

As I grew older, my stories grew and I began to argue with everyone about almost anything. Desperately, I tried to justify my thinking in order to feel equal and important. My self-esteem was so low that it was almost non-existent.

Without realizing it, I was getting what I wanted. I was obtaining the result of the seeds I had planted in my subconscious by constantly repeating the negative affirmations: *no one loves me; no one cares; I'll never amount to a hill of beans!* I later learned that I was actually speaking things into existence that I did not want.

• • •

DALE CARNEGIE

At the age of seventeen, I enrolled in the Dale Carnegie course to gain self-confidence, to become a good speaker, and to learn more about human nature. Really? Sounds good, but that is not the reason I enrolled.

I was a high school distributive education student at the time. I went to school half of the day and worked in a family shoe store the

THE POWER OF SELF-IMAGING

other half. I took the Dale Carnegie course because my boss told me that if I did not take the course I would lose my job. It was that simple.

He recognized the fact that my argumentative nature was due to negative subconscious programming. He believed the course would help me see the possibilities for change that could lead to a much brighter future. He was trying to help me improve. He was hoping I would soon see the stupidity of my actions

He too had similar challenges in his life and had taken the Dale Carnegie course right after being discharged from the Army, where he served as a drill instructor, better known to military folks as a DI. People who have been in the military and have gone through boot camp know what DI's do and the unconventional methods they use to make changes in the life of new recruits.

The DI's job is to mentally and physically tear the recruit down and destroy his negative view of himself, to cure the *I can't disease*. It is the DI's job to rebuild his/her physical body and self-esteem in order to create a warrior with a *can do* attitude and program a soldier to automatically follow orders. If you are a soldier and your sergeant tells you to hit the dirt, you don't ask why, you just do what you're told and you do it immediately.

I had no money. Due to the fact that I was paid seven percent commissions, with a minimum guarantee of twelve dollars and fifty cents per week, my income fluctuated. There was no way to borrow the one hundred and eighty dollars that it took to enroll in the course, so I went to visit the instructor in his hotel room, hoping to arrange for payment over the life of the course. I was very nervous and ashamed to ask, but he not only agreed, he personally guaranteed (not part of the Dale Carnegie guarantee) that if I didn't double my income during the sixteen weeks, he would refund my money. How could I go wrong?

I've always believed my employer knew the instructor and had asked him to help me. Although I don't know for sure, my employer probably guaranteed payment for the course as well. I was argumentative, but I was hard worker and wanted to learn the shoe business. I had a strong desire to succeed, so if taking the Dale Carnegie course was going to help me keep my job, double my income and help me succeed, where do I sign?

After a few classes, I began to see the light. I realized the course had the potential to help me, but it was up to me to change. I hoped the course would change the direction of my life, as my boss and the instructor said it would. Most of all, I hoped it would help me learn how to be accepted by others, which is something that I had missed all my life. At age seventeen that was a full plate. I was the youngest student in a class of thirty-four.

• • •

THE ONE-MINUTE SPEECH
It was just a one-minute speech and it really felt good to hear the audience applaud and say, "Great job! Nice speech!" The instructor agreed and praised me in front of the whole class. WOW! It felt great. Sincere praise was mine for the first time that I could remember. I felt important and was anxious to learn more and to do even better.

After complimenting me, my instructor and classmates pointed to areas in the speech where I could make improvements. I heard corrective criticism, as they called it, and for once I did not resent being corrected. It motivated me to do better. I even won a few prizes for giving the best speech and for being the most improved speaker.

As I read the words in Dale Carnegie's book, *How to Win Friends and Influence People,* I realized he was talking to me. He says, "Make the other person feel important—and do it sincerely."

William James, an 18th century psychologist referred to as the father of American Psychology, said, "The deepest principle in human nature is the craving to be appreciated." How true! Finally, someone was doing just that—making me feel important and appreciated. I was beginning to feel like somebody.

While taking the Dale Carnegie course, and realizing some of the errors of my ways, I began a search for answers to some of life's most profound questions. I began to realize that it was not too late for me.

I discovered that for things to get better for me, I had to change. I learned that I had no control over other people, but I did have control over myself.

I realized I could read the biographies and learn what others had done. I could search for answers on my own, teach myself and ask questions without feeling ignorant. I learned to say, "I am sorry," "I am wrong," and most of all I realized, I was already somebody. With all the excitement of a child in a toy store, I became a seeker.

Not only did the Dale Carnegie course help me double my income, I actually tripled my income through sales commissions. I was earning a much higher income by applying the human relations techniques that I had learned in the course.

I had learned to take my eyes off myself and put them on other people—to see things from their point of view. It was amazing! People were finally treating me with respect.

With this newly found hope, I wanted to know what motivates people do what they do, say what they say, and turn out being the way they are. What is success? What are the real secrets of life? What keeps people from taking action? I thought, "There must be secrets I am not yet aware of for achieving success."

In my search for what makes the difference in every area of my life, I discovered *people always get what they want*. And, amazingly, I discovered that words become things. The words I chose to say to myself became life choices, and these choices had become my reality. No wonder my life had been such a mess!

• • •

THE SETUP

Whether you realize it or not, your choices and the actions you take because of those choices are affecting the lives of people all over the world. You may believe that your thoughts and the actions you take because of those thoughts are so small and insignificant that they will have no effect at all, but the law of the universe states that it is impossible to transform energy without eventually affecting the whole of the universe.

For every action (small or large) there is an equal but opposite reaction. It is how the Spirit of the Universe set things up. The laws of the universe were established so that all things would work together for good. These laws include the laws of energy, cause and effect, gravity, the law of motion, and the Chaos Theory, also referred to as the butterfly effect.

The law of motion states that an object in motion tends to remain in motion until stopped by an outside force. The simplified law of gravity says, if you pitch the ball up, it will come down. If you jump from a building you will not fall up, you will fall down. Learn the setup!

The butterfly effect is a term used in the Chaos Theory to describe how tiny variations, such as the flapping of butterfly wings, can affect giant complex weather systems throughout the world. The tiny variations in a weather pattern could theoretically cause tornadoes halfway around the world.

The law of *cause and effect* is a universal scientific law. It does not care if you believe it or not. It is part of the setup, and it works no matter where you are in the entire universe. It says that nothing happens by chance and that *everything happens for a reason.*

The choices (action) we make, no matter if they come from conscious or subconscious thought, will cause equal and corresponding opposite affects. If you touch (action) a hot skillet, you will get burned (reaction). If you pitch (action) the ball up, the ball will fall (reaction) down to earth.

Whatever thoughts you have and whatever actions you take will come back to you. You always get back what you send out and quiet often more abundantly. One of the most powerful things about this law that works in your favor is that when your thoughts are focused on specific goals, you always get *what you have to have,* even more abundantly. When you plant a tomato see, you don't get just one tomato, do you? You get many tomatoes! Be careful what you plant.

Affirmation 4

I am constantly on guard and aware of the thoughts in my conscious mind.

I am aware of free will consequences.

I am aware that choices become things; therefore, I will shed the negative choices that lead me away from my life purpose.

I am aware that the actions I take touch the lives of people all over the world.

I am discarding thoughts that are not based on purity of intent and integrity.

I am honest with myself, and the world.

I am aware of the law of cause and effect; therefore, I guard my thoughts.

10
It Starts on the Inside

We can do only what we think we can do. We can be only what we think we can be. We can have only what we think we can have. What we do, what we are, what we have, all depend upon what we think.

—**Robert Collier**

AS A YOUNG man I dreamed of being wealthy and powerful. I would own of all kinds of wonderful toys and other material possessions. Deep inside, without realizing it, what I really wanted was recognition, power, happiness, self worth, and peace of mind. I was not aware that thoughts become things.

Of course, I naturally assumed money, recognition, and position would bring me the happiness, peace of mind, and power I was seeking; but, I had no idea how much money, power, and recognition it would take before I could finally reach my 'live happily ever after' status. My assumption was whatever that amount was had to be significantly huge.

Like most people, I only had vague ideas, which were mostly just daydreams. Playing the *I wish I had, I wish I could,* and *one day I will* game, I hoped that someone would give me the chance to be somebody. I was searching on the outside of myself and depending on others to bring me the success I desired. I did not know I could choose to be happy.

People are constantly looking for happiness as though it is some object that can't be found. Some look for happiness in strange places—in the ownership of things, in relationships, in drugs, in alcohol, in hobbies, and in personal accomplishments—without realizing happiness is a choice.

We can choose to be happy or we can choose to be depressed, fearful, and unhappy. It really is our choice. Happiness is an inside job.

Man is about as happy as he makes up his mind to be.

—Abraham Lincoln

Happiness is not wrapped up in financial success, big fancy cars, a big home, and world travel. Although there is nothing wrong with having a large home and nice cars, they are only delusions. Once you have the big house you'll soon discover that it is just another house. When you finally buy that car you've always dreamed of owning, after a while you will realize that it is just another car. It is great to have nice things, but things are just that, things...your stuff. While the ownership of cool stuff is okay and may even give you a sensation of happiness, in reality you cannot achieve true happiness through the ownership of things.

While ego will try to convince you otherwise, other people don't care how big your house is, what car you drive, or how much money you have. They really don't care what you look like or how you dress. The average person won't recall what clothes you wore yesterday, and they probably won't recall much of what you said during what you considered to be an interesting conversation.

Average people only care about what *they* say. They care about what *they* look like, what house *they* live in, what kind of car *they* drive. They listen to themselves more deeply than they do to what you have to say. That is one of the main reasons most people can't remember names.

While they are introducing themselves, people (unaware) concentrate more on hearing their own name rather than listening to the name of a new acquaintance. Dale Carnegie said, "Remember that a person's name is to that person the sweetest and most important sound in any language."

Most people are more concerned with themselves. It is an ego thing. Ego makes sure we are aware of how great we are and how wonderful we look.

Even when the newness of a possession wears off and reality sets in, we still find it difficult to understand that the ownership of things does not provide our long-term happiness. Sure, all that great stuff may make us feel good for a while, but we already have the happiness we seek. We don't need material things to satisfy that need. We only need to stop and be grateful for the gifts we already have been given and realize that all the gold in Fort Knox cannot make us happy. In today's economy having money is good thing. It serves us well within the area in which it is designed to serve, but it is not the end-all for happiness, and does not spell success. We only need to make up our mind that from now on we will choose to be happy, regardless of circumstances.

The challenge of pursuing personal goals that include material things is part of the fun things that we do in life, but we need to remember that reaching goals is what we do. It is not *who* we are.

It is difficult to be unhappy when you have a smile on your face. Go look in a mirror and smile. If you don't feel like smiling, do it anyway. Put a smile on your face. I'll bet you can't look at your body in the mirror without smiling. Try it right now. Notice and experience how you feel emotionally when you smile.

While feeling happy is a wonderful thing, we should remember that it is an emotion. The feeling of happiness comes and goes. Happiness ebbs and flows with the words we say to ourselves. Be

THE POWER OF SELF-IMAGING

consciously aware of your thoughts at all times. No matter the ebb and flow of your emotions, realize that happiness is always with you... on the inside.

Most people never try to achieve the desires of the heart or find true happiness simply because they perceive their chances of success as unreachable. They develop the, *I can't disease* and continue to live in their settled-for comfort zone.

What would our lives be like if Henry Ford, Alexander Graham Bell, Benjamin Franklin, Thomas Edison, Isaac Newton, Albert Einstein, Bill Gates, Steve Jobs, to name a few, had perceived failure instead of success?

• • •

WISHING AND DREAMING
Many times as a young boy, I remember sitting on the front porch at my grandfather's farmhouse listening to the grown-ups casually talking about this and that, mostly about the crops, money, or "I wish I'da."

I remember my uncle leaning back against the old frame house in a cane bottomed chair saying, "Ya know, if I'da bought that piece of land down thar next to old Buford's place a few years back, it would be worth a lotta money right now. I could've bought that 300 acres for $3.00 an acre back then. Today it's worth $10.00 an acre. Can ye believe that? Seems the price of things jest keep getting higher and higher."

"Yeah, that's right!" Papa said, as he lay in his squeaky porch swing rocking back and forth, picking his teeth with a broom straw. "I had a chance to git that land myself and passed it up. Ye know, I could've bought that 100 acres over thar across the road. I guess I should've, but ya know how tis; I need every dime I can rake up to make my crops. Prices keep going up, but I ain't seen no benefit yet."

Sitting there, I listened to every word and mentally joined in the chorus of, "I wish I'da, would've, could've, should've."

It seems week after week they sang the same song. It was as though they had forgotten what they talked about the last time.

Occasionally, the conversation would veer off to something new that they saw or heard about somewhere. Most often it was something they saw in the Sears Roebuck or Montgomery Ward catalog while visiting the outhouse down the path behind the house. The conversations always seemed to end with, "Wish I could afford to buy jest one thang in them catalogs."

No doubt they were just wishing and dreaming of things they believed might bring a little more pleasure and happiness, without realizing they were already living a life that millions of other people throughout the world hungered for. Compared to the vast majority of people in the world, they were already wealthy and, as I remember it, very happy as well.

What people really mean when they say "You can't go around living in a dream world" is "I don't believe I can do it, so I don't believe you can do it either". They don't realize that *everything starts with a dream*, a dream that has been preordained and given to them.

• • •

LIVING IN A DREAM WORLD

John calls himself a realist. "I live in the real world. Dreaming about things you know you are never going to do, just get you all worked up for nothing. Sometimes you just have to tell yourself the truth and admit you ain't so smart. You need to do what you know, and leave the rest to somebody else. You know…you just have to keep your feet on the ground and your head out of the clouds. Someday I'll succeed at something. It just ain't hit me yet."

He doesn't attempt to set goals because he has been programmed to believe he can't succeed. He has the, *I can't disease*. John does not know his future is preordained. The, *I can't disease* just slows down progress.

There are no foolish goals. No matter what others may think, you will choose the goals that have been established for you by the Spirit of the Universe.

• • •

GOD KNOWS YOUR SECRETS
In the *Holy Bible*, 1 Corinthians: 2: 9-12, Paul teaches us:

> That is what the Scriptures mean when they say, no eye has seen, no ear has heard; no mind has conceived what **God has prepared** for those who love him. But God has revealed it to us by his Spirit. The Spirit searches all things, even the deep things of God. *For who among men knows the thoughts of a man except the man's spirit within him.* In the same way no one knows the thoughts of God except the Spirit of God. We have not received the spirit of the world but the Spirit who is from God, that we may understand what God has freely given us.

The Spirit of God lives in us and speaks to us daily through our thoughts. All we have to do is be quite and listen.

• • •

VOICES IN OUR HEAD
One evening my daughter Pamela, her husband Gordon, and our granddaughter Bianca, dropped by to visit for a while. We decided to order pizza, and I volunteered to go pick it up. Bianca, who was seven-years-old at the time, rode with me to get the pizza. I thought the time would be well spent bonding with her.

She was quieter than usual that evening. Trying to get a conversation going, I asked, "Do you ever have a conversation with yourself? Like thinking things through in your head?"

She looked at me with that 'deer in the headlights' look in her eyes and no doubt wondered why I would ask such a question. I explained, "Everyone talks to themselves. As a matter of fact, we talk to ourselves most of the time."

She said, "Yes, I guess. You mean like when I am thinking and not talking? I do that all the time."

Being as careful as possible not to confuse her, I said, "We have good thoughts that tell us the right thing to do and we occasionally have bad thought's that encourage us to do bad things. Sometimes those thoughts get kind of confusing. Do you hear voices that tell you to do things?" She didn't know how to respond.

"Let's pretend like there is a little person that sits on your right shoulder talking to you in your right ear. You can't see it, but it talks to you all the time. Let's call this little person 'Good'. It tells you the right choices to make as you go about your daily activities."

"Then there is a little person that sits on your left shoulder, always talking to you in your left ear. Let's name this little person on your left shoulder 'Evil' because it is always trying to take you down the wrong path. Evil will tell you to lie and steal. Evil might even get you into a fight and make you harm someone. Evil will try to convince you that you will not get caught, that nothing will happen."

"Evil will tell you that you don't need to study and that you are already smart enough. When you get a bit older Evil may tell you to take drugs, or get drunk on whisky or beer. Evil might even convince you to rob someone or to kill someone in order to get money to buy more drugs or alcohol. Evil is VERY bad!"

"Evil knows that Good is on your right shoulder and he hates Good. Evil is an expert at choosing just the right words to encourage you to do the wrong thing. Evil will disguise his voice and sound just like Good's voice in order to make you think you are making the right choice."

"Every time Good makes a suggestion, Evil will try to contradict it. When Good tells you something, Evil will say things like, "Don't believe that. Nothing is going to happen to you. How will anyone know?" All the while, the Good voice is begging you to do the right thing."

"Do you ever hear those voices talking to you?" I asked.

"Yes...I...I think I do...sometimes. I hear, but sometimes I listen to the one on this shoulder and I get in trouble," she said, pointing to her left shoulder.

"Yes, Evil is really bad. If you want to be good and do good things, always listen to Good that is on your right shoulder and tell Evil to leave you alone," I concluded.

After an evening of pizza and a few laughs, our granddaughter went home with her parents. It had not been more than fifteen minutes or so when I received a phone call from Bianca.

"Papaw, Papaw," she cried.

"What's wrong, Babe?" I asked.

"Papaw, I can't remember which shoulder the Good voice is on." And so it is with lots of folks. We're often not sure what to listen to.

We had a good laugh about that. She didn't say so, but I would guess Ben, her big brother, was bothering her again and she wanted to retaliate.

All success and happiness comes from choosing to listen to the Good voice, the voice that says, "I can," "I am somebody," "God loves me." It all starts on the inside.

Affirmation 5
I am aware of the voices that speak to me.
 I am living a life of positive choice.
 I am aware that if I have an attitude of anger, and sadness, my life will be filled with pessimism.
 I am aware that when I am filled with negativity and pessimism these attitudes follow me where ever I go.
 I choose to bring happiness, enthusiasm, and an attitude filled with laughter and joy so that those I meet will react with joy, enthusiasm, happiness and laughter.
 I am the captain of my emotions.

11
The Comfort Zone

Nature has placed humanity under the government of two sovereign masters, pain and pleasure. They govern us in all we do, in all we say, in all we think. Every effort we can make to throw off our subjection will serve but to demonstrate and confirm it.

—Jeremy Bentham

OFTEN PEOPLE GET caught up in reactive behavior, trying to put out fires that have already burned. They feel trapped by self-inflicted financial constraints, believing life has dealt them a bad hand. They don't believe they are at fault for making poor choices. Instead they create self-authored stories that provide justification for any poor choices they may have made in order to make themselves look good. In their mind they have been given a bad hand to play and there is nothing they can do about it. Eventually they settle for what becomes their comfort zone, which is somewhere just below their highest achievement in life. The zone usually encompasses much less than they had once hoped for.

A comfort zone can be a place, a space, or a point of physical and mental comfort. It can be a career, a position, or an income level. A comfort zone can be all these and more, all of which are mental zones designed by and enhanced by our own self-talk.

It is obvious that many people do succeed financially and have great life styles; however, for the vast majority, success is just being able to hold on to a job. Like sheep, they follow the flock into an open-ended grave—life's rut.

• • •

THE LIFE OF JOHN
Bill Britt, entrepreneur and highly successful businessman says in a taped speech (paraphrasing):

> Monday morning at six, John slowly removes himself from bed, dreading the thought of having to go to a job he hates. He wonders what challenges the week will bring his way.
>
> He eats breakfast, gets dressed and leaves for work, arriving close to eight o'clock. Around ten that morning he takes a coffee break and visits with his co-workers in the break-room. They talk about how bad things are in the world, at home and on the job. At noon he goes to lunch. About three that afternoon he takes another coffee break, where again he talks about everything that's wrong with the world, and maybe sports and work. John returns to his cubicle and halfheartedly concentrates on the project at hand.
>
> At five that afternoon, on the dot, he leaves the office, finds his car and makes his way through the hour-long bumper-to-bumper traffic until he finally arrives home, where, hopefully, dinner is waiting for him. He eats his evening meal on a tray in front of the television and watches TV until ten o'clock and then goes to his bedroom, where he has another television. He falls asleep watching the evening news.

On Tuesday things are going to be different. This day John gets up, eats a little breakfast, goes to work, takes a coffee break, eats lunch, takes another coffee break, goes home, eats dinner, watches a little TV, and goes to bed.

On Wednesday—thank God! It's almost Friday. The weekend is going to be so great. Today things are going to be different. He gets up, eats a little breakfast, goes to work, takes a coffee break, eats lunch, takes another coffee break, goes home, eats dinner, watches a little TV, and goes to bed, where he falls asleep watching the ten o'clock news. And so it goes! Without realizing it, John is just another sheep in the flock.

John tends to live his life based on what he perceives to be true and how things are suppose to be. After all, this is the way his father and grandfather, and most of his friends live.

Financial success eludes him because he lives in the self-created illusion that he can't succeed financially. He believes that wealth (his idea of success) is only meant for a certain group of people, and that group does not include him. John has settled for his position among the sheep and the fleas of the world.

• • •

HOW TO TRAIN A FLEA
Some people live their life like trained fleas. How are fleas trained? Pick up a few fleas off a yard dog and put them in a jar. Punch a few holes in the lid and then watch them jump. If they don't jump, just shake the jar a little and watch what happens. Bosses know how this works.

The fleas will begin to sense danger. They feel trapped so they will try to jump out. They want to be free. They will jump and jump, but they keep hitting their head on the lid. It finally occurs to them that they can't get out.

After a while, they will give up trying. At that point the lid can be removed. The fleas will continue to jump, but just so high, not realizing the lid is off. They could escape if they wanted to, but they have been trained to believe they cannot. Most people are a lot like fleas!

Elephants are trained in a similar manner. When the elephant is a baby, the trainer, careful to position the baby a short distance from its mom, will attach one end of a strong chain around one of its legs and then attach the other end of the chain around the trunk of a tree or a similar strong or stable object. The trainer knows the baby will try hard to go to the comfort and safety of its mom. The baby will pull as hard as it can, trying to get free, but it cannot break the chain. It will keep trying until the pain is more than it can bear.

After a while it occurs to the elephant that it cannot get free, so it quits trying. When this occurs, the chain may be replaced with a strong rope. The rope is then tied to a metal stake that has been driven into the ground. The elephant could easily pull free, but once it feels resistance it will not attempt to pull free. It has been programmed to believe it cannot free itself.

Most people are programmed to believe they can't. They've hit their head on the lid and pulled on the chain until they get the *I can't disease*, a severe mental condition brought on by self-talk. Soon they settle into their comfort zone.

For years I lived my life as a flea in the jar. It was easy to keep me in line. All my superiors had to do to get me to do what they wanted was to shake the jar a little. I quickly fell into place and looked for the small space where I was not easily noticed. I had jumped as high as I believed I could. I had tried as hard as I thought I could to succeed, but each time I tried to get free I hit my head on the lid.

I finally reached a point in my life where I discovered the truth. The lid was open and I could get free. I was not an elephant and I was not a flea. I was free to do whatever I wanted to do. I was not concerned, worried, or fearful of what could happen to me in the process of going for my dreams.

Nothing could have been worse than believing I was trapped. When my eyes were finally opened, I came to realize that for things to get better for me I had to look on the inside. I had to change.

For things to change for you, you must climb out of your comfort zone. Remember, you are not a flea. The lid is open. You can pull up the stake. Your choices are on the inside!

We tend to get what we expect. If we expect to do well, we usually do. If we expect to fail, surely we will get what we expect. Someone once said, "He who expects nothing shall not be disappointed."

People are not forced into their comfort zones. They have designed their own comfort zone by the choices they've made. They remain there because they believe nothing will ever change, that things will always be the same, so why bother. They believe they have no other choice. They feel they are not worthy of anything more. They have hit their head on the lid.

If this is how you feel, you may have a case of the *I can't disease*.

Just remember this: a rubber band will never serve its designed purpose until it is stretched.

Affirmation 6
I am a unique creature personally designed by God, the Spirit of the Universe.
    I am not a flea, an elephant or a sheep.
    I am filled with the Spirit of God and guided by His will.
    I am living a life of great expectation.
    In stillness, within me, where God abides, I hear His voice. I feel His presence.
    I am consciously aware of ego and its desire to control my life. I cast away ego's thoughts of superiority and greed.
    I recognize failure for what it really is—God working in me to take away those things that will keep me from achieving His preordained purpose in my life.
    I know that for every failure or setback that I experience, God has prepared blessings far greater than I can imagine.
    I am seeking His daily guidance.
    I expect miracles.

12
Choices

We make decisions, and then our decisions turn around and make us.

—F. W. Boreham

IT IS AMAZING how, when we are searching for answers, God seems to place us in just the right place at the right time to stretch our minds and to pull us out of our comfort zone—that open ended grave we've become so acquainted with.

As I look back on events in my life, I see more clearly now that the purpose for many negative events that seemed to happen for no apparent reason turned out in my favor. I did not realize events resulted from choices I had made, either directly or indirectly. Being required to take the Dale Carnegie Course was one of those events. It was a choice made for me, but a choice I readily chose to accept. And it was a life changing choice.

That first evening of the Dale Carnegie course, the instructor asked four attendees at a time to sit on top of a 4 X 6 folding table he had provided. The purpose was to make us feel comfortable and relaxed as we introduced ourselves to the class.

The class of thirty-four was made up of people from all walk's of life: bankers, attorneys, plumbers, housewives, teachers, route salesperson, a milkman, a fry cook, restaurant owners, and sales people. They were people just like me who needed to make changes in their lives.

While I was waiting my turn to introduce myself, I kept asking myself, "What have I done? What am I doing here? Why did I decide to do this?" I wanted to leave. I wanted to tell the instructor to leave me out of this part. I thought, "I do not want to do this." I was petrified!

I was not sure what kind of miracles this course would provide. I only knew I had to take the course and, for this to work for me, I would need to stretch my mind to a new scary dimension. I was shaking and not sure what to do or say.

There should have been no reason for me to be nervous or scared. After all, the other class members must have been just as scared.

"Tell us about yourself, who you are, what you do, and what you expect to gain from taking this course," the instructor said.

When it finally came my turn I thought I would die. I could barely speak. I can still recall that experience. Nervously, I said, as I attempted to tell the audience who I was, "My name is Joel Johnson. I live here in Tyler, Texas. I am a student at Tyler High School and I am in the eleventh grade. I am a Distributive Education student. I go to school the first half of the school day and work the other half in a family shoe store, where I am a shoe salesman, a stock clerk and a window trimmer. I am interested in the retail business as a future career."

"I was born in Teaselville, Texas, which is about ten miles south of Tyler. I spent my first few years on a farm and moved to Tyler when I was around nine years old."

"My father is a fireman for the Tyler Fire Department and on his days off he is a carpenter. He does not put up with much from us kids (a few chuckles). My mother is a housewife. I have one brother and three sisters, and we all live at home with our parents."

"The reason I am taking this course is because my boss told me that if I didn't take this course, I could not work for him."

"He tells me I argue too much, talk too much, and my big sister tells everyone I am a big know-it-all (more laughter)."

"I would like to learn more about myself, and I would like to learn how to communicate without arguing or having people think bad things of me."

Although it only took a little over thirty seconds to introduce myself, it seemed like an eternity, and I was astonished that it turned out as well as it did.

As I look back on that evening at the Blackstone Hotel in Tyler, Texas, I will never forget the faces in the audience. Everyone seemed so attentive and interested. They seemed to hang onto every word I said, and yet it was only a simple introduction that included the use of the words "I" way too many times.

My ego was applauding inside me for having made it through that episode. It did not want anyone to know about the secrets I kept hidden in the back of my mental closet—my subconscious.

It did not want them to know that I believed my dad hated me; that no one loved me; that I was ignorant; that I was a poor student; that I was a cat killer; that *I would never amount to a hill of beans*; or that I was wasting my time taking the Dale Carnegie course, to name a few. It wanted me to look good. All of these things I chose to believe about myself, none of which were actually true.

For the Dale Carnegie course to work for me, I realized that I had to change my attitude. I discovered that it was not just those around me who needed to change. If things were going to change in my life, I had to make a personal choice to change.

During the course, I developed an eager desire to know more about how to make friends and influence people. I wanted to know how the choices I had made had brought me to this point in my life. I wanted to understand more deeply how things work in a world. The answers to these questions and more are in books. I began reading.

• • •

BOOKS OF GOLD

As I read biographies of the highly successful people portrayed in Dale Carnegie's book, *How to Win Friends and Influence People*, I began to wonder why some people from poverty stricken environments, and with very little formal education, achieve financial success beyond their wildest imagination, while others with access to capital, educated and from affluent backgrounds quite often failed to even try. It obviously was their choice, but why?

As a naive young man I wondered if anyone had really researched these questions. I visited the public library to see what had been discovered over the past several decades concerning human relations and motivation. Sure enough, there they were—hundreds of books filled with the answers I was seeking. I began to read and read. I couldn't get the information fast enough. Through reading I was exposed to many secrets of the universe, secrets of classic writers, and spiritual teachers.

Jim Rohn says (paraphrasing):

> Books are like an ocean filled with gold and people don't read them. You want to say to non-readers, "Hey John, come on down, look at all this gold. Bring your shovel and a bucket and come get you some. There is more gold here than I will ever need."
>
> John answers, "I don't have a bucket."
>
> Roan said, "Well...go get you one."
>
> John says, "Do you know how much they want for buckets and shovels?"
>
> And John is behind! He's broke! He can't pay his rent or his car payment and he can't figure out why! HE'S BEHIND! BEHIND! Can you believe that?

To find the answers, be a seeker. Make the right choices. Read the books, attend the seminars, listen to the audios, watch the DVDs, study—it's all there. Everything you will ever want to know is available to you in books, e-books, podcasts, and videos on the Internet. There is no excuse!

Books help you learn the rules of life. When you learn God's rules (the *setup)*, you will make better choices. You might even discover the unused portion of your creative genius and the untapped power within you.

Reading stimulates the power of the human brain and its potential. Why not learn how powerful you really are? Why not learn the potential of your own brain? Why not learn how it works?

The human brain is the most amazing instrument in the entire universe, yet we humans know very little about how it works. As an example, Susan A. Greenfield, in her book, *The Human Brain*, says, "Consider just the outer layer of the brain, the cortex. If you counted the connections between neurons in this outer layer at a rate of one connection a second, it would take thirty-two million years!"

Here is another good example of how powerful the brain is. In his book, *How the Brain Works*, Leslie H. Hart offers an example of what goes on mentally when someone is simply dancing. He says, "Every second, hundreds of thousands of bits of information stream into the brain reporting where various muscles are, what stresses are on them, and what changes are in progress, plus reports on conditions in many other systems that must respond to the extra effort of trying to dance. This flood of simultaneous input to be analyzed, evaluated, and coordinated in real time without appreciable delay would bring the largest manmade computer to a gibbering breakdown from overload."

Because you have one of these amazing things called a human brain, you have the ability to make the right choices.

The goal oriented subconscious mind, the creative mind that is housed within your brain, is impersonal. The subconscious mind automatically works to create success and happiness, or unhappiness and failure, depending upon your choices. The subconscious mind does not care—garbage in, garbage out. It will do whatever you ask.

> *Present your creative mechanism with 'successful goals', and it functions as a success mechanism. Present it with negative goals, and it operates just as impersonally, and just as faithfully as a failure mechanism.*
>
> —Dr. Maxwell Maltz, M. D., F.I.C.S.

• • •

BRAINSTORMING

While searching for answers on how choices evolve and where ideas come from, I learned that ideas created by this automatic goal oriented mechanism, (the brain) is responsible for every aspect of our lives. I learned that in the process of brainstorming, astonishing new ideas emerge from this real and very powerful force within the brain.

Have you ever noticed that while talking to someone about planning, problem solving, or in just normal conversations, ideas that you've not even thought of before just seem to pop up out of nowhere? This is the creative mind at work. When two or more are gathered in conversation or prayer, this third mind seems to hover in midair, unnoticed and invisible offering it's perspective on ideas, methods, and offering solutions to complex challenges.

Every nanosecond the subconscious mind absorbs millions of bits of information, while creating the *mental movie* of your life. Each frame contains your perception and interpretation of events as they happen.

The subconscious retains and never forgets even the smallest detail. Past thoughts and events may lay dormant for long periods of time; nonetheless, they still remain in the subconscious. You could casually notice a spot on a wall in your peripheral vision and several years later, with the right stimulus, recall that spot and the events that occurred when you first observed it.

The choices we make are derived from mental programming and self-talk. We are programmed to believe we can do this or that or we cannot do this or that by what we hear, observe, perceive and interpret. Our unconscious choices confuse what we consciously perceive as reality. We are programmed to believe that many of the things that happen to us are simply out of our control.

I hate to be the one to burst your bubble, and yes un-planned things do happen, things that you could not perceive, but are nonetheless preordained to happen. You must realize it was you who made the choice to be at that location, inside that car when you were rear-ended. You made the choice to be in that particular restaurant when the gunman came in and shot up the place. You chose to buy the airline ticket and you chose to board that plane that crashed. You didn't deliberately choose to put yourself in harm's way, but you did consciously make the choice to be there. Had you not made those choices, you would be seeing those events in the news instead of being what you perceive as the victim. Everything happens for a reason.

You have chosen to read this book. Life is full of choices, one after another. Not choosing is also a choice. There are consequences involved in every choice, good and bad.

Jesus said, "Whatsoever you soweth, that shall you also reap." Another reality is, you will reap more abundantly, whether you have made good choices or bad choices. The law does not care. The law says you will reap more than you plant. Be careful what you plant.

What do you say to yourself? Are you building yourself up or putting yourself down? What you say to yourself and how you respond to that information sets the pace for your current and future life, more abundantly. Your thoughts create and control your emotions. Your emotions, how you feel about things, determine the choices you make.

Happiness is a *choice*, a state of mind. Happiness is not in the achievement of great things; happiness is in the pursuit of great things. Happiness is not found in arriving, it is found in the journey. It is not the having that counts, it is being alive in the present moment—in the *doing, being* and *becoming*—that brings true happiness. That kind of happiness you already have on the inside of you.

It is a choice not based on outside influences. Often the things that deny your happiness are compressed negative memories tucked away in your subconscious. Self-talk reaffirms your interpretation of those memories.

Affirmation 7
I am conscious of the fact that if allowed, ego would have me perceive a false reality.

I am the observer and the actor. I am the seer and the doer. I can choose to sit in the audience and watch the play or I can choose to be in the play, on the field, and in the action, where all of life exists.

I am visualizing the final results before taking the first step toward fruition.

I am successful.

13
Suppression/Compression and Sensory Reality

Our brains give us only an approximate view of reality, because they mix new knowledge with past memories and store them together as one.

—John Medina

YOU DON'T HAVE to say "save as" to have your thoughts and actions saved on your mental hard drive. It is automatic. Your thoughts and actions are sorted and filed away in the subconscious to be recalled and used according to your preordained life purpose.

Traumatic thoughts and actions are hidden away (suppressed) for your own benefit. A mother may remember that she had horrible pains during labor and childbirth; a man lost his leg in an auto accident; a soldier was shot; but they cannot recall the actual pain itself because the brain causes the subconscious mind to immediately suppress it.

Psychiatrists and psychologists use the word *suppressed* when describing a memory that the subconscious deliberately withholds from conscious recall. The fact that a memory cannot be recalled does not mean the memory is not stored away in the subconscious mind. It is simply hidden from conscious memory.

Memory of some medical procedures can be artificially suppressed with the use of drugs administered by an anesthesiologist during surgery. You can remember that you had a procedure, but you cannot remember the pain or events that occurred during the procedure.

Traumatic experiences such as child molestation, murder, attempted suicide, adultery, rape, rage, theft, child beatings, mental and physical abuses, are often consciously compressed (deliberately hidden). They are not suppressed in the same sense as pain. Compressed memories are negative events that we can easily recall, but we would rather not think about or talk about. We keep these memories locked away in the back of our mental closet and they become mental baggage. Many of these compressed memories hidden away in the back of our mental closet are events that have the potential to hold us back as we seek to find our life purpose.

A traumatic experience can easily occur while a person is dreaming, or it may occur when a person is simply witnessing a horrible event. It can happen deep within the subconscious mind while a person is watching a traumatic event in a movie or on television. The subconscious mind does not know the difference between what is real and what is not or between what is true or what is false.

Most of what you believe to be true about yourself and the events that you perceive as real is based on how things occur to you in context. With close examination of the facts, you will discover that your perception of the world in which you live is mostly an illusion.

Even our sensory system (taste, smell, touch, sight, and hearing) that helps us navigate through this mysterious world we call reality can be called in as suspect.

We have been taught and mentally programmed to believe that the real world exists out there somewhere. Of course, it does. However, in reality each person experiences his/her own existence in his/her own brain. Therefore, what I experience in my world is dramatically different from what you experience in your world.

You might discover with extensive study that your perception of things in the universe is not as it seems to be. For instance, the eminent British neurologist, Sir John C. Eccles pierced the sensory illusion with one startling but irrefutable assertion when he says, "I want you to realize that there is *no color* in the *natural world* and *no sound*—nothing of this kind; *no textures, no patterns, no beauty, no scent*. In short, none of the objective facts upon which we usually base our reality is fundamentally valid."

The sensory nerve system can be compared to millions of microscopic computers located throughout the human form that are connected directly to the spinal chord and then to the brain. The sensory nerve system acts as the perceptive window to our individual worlds. It tells us what is, as our mind perceives things to be.

No one really knows how much information one neuron holds. It is believed the cerebral cortex (the outer layer of the brain) may contain twenty billion or more neurons—tiny neuronal computers more powerful than any man made computer to date.

Even with our massive potential brain power and our ability to analyze the information absorbed on a daily basis, we unconsciously continue to be programmed by other people and by our own interpretations of life's events. Scientists are beginning to understand, though slowly, how the human brain reads, understands, and analyzes written texts.

The legend, propagated by email and message boards, purportedly demonstrates that readers can understand the meaning of words in a sentence even when the interior letters of each word are scrambled. As long as all the necessary letters are present, and the first and last letters remain the same, readers appear to have little trouble reading the text.

The creation of such email messages started with a letter to the New Scientist Magazine from Graham Rawlinson of Nottingham

University in which he discusses his Ph.D. thesis, suggesting keeping the first and last two letters of each word in place.

According to the Internet organization *Wikipedia.org*:

> Typoglycemia is a neologism given to a purported recent discovery about the cognitive processes behind reading written text. The word appears to be a portmanteau of "typo", as in typographical error, and "hypoglycemia". It is an urban legend/Internet meme that appears to have an element of truth to it.

Example: Read the following paragraphs and see if you understand what is written.

Smoe momires are hrad to rcaell wehn tehy are not ipmortnet to us or tehy are not egxagraeted eunogh; hwoveer, momires of taramitc envtes are nveer lsot.

If you wnat to rmebmer nmeas, fcaes, ojcbets and ohetr tinhgs, bolw tehm up out of perproiton wtih mneatl eagxgretaion.

When we read or hear words, a picture of the subject automatically enters our mind. Those pictures determine our perception of events within context. What we perceive to be true about our environment and ourselves is not always based on real facts, but rather on perceived facts.

Remember, the subconscious mind does not know the difference between what is real, imaginary, or false. It acts or fails to act based on what it imagines to be true about the environment, and events that occur.

Having some sense of how the mind and brain works helps create powerful affirmations that will move you to your preordained purpose in life.

Affirmation 8
I am aware that words contain the power to change my world.
 I am guarding my words.
 I am consciousness, the spirit entity within, one with the Spirit of the Universe, the observer of all things, the controller of all events; therefore, rest assured that what is preordained for me to experience, I will experience and what is not preordained for me to experience, I will not experience.
 I cannot fail.

14
The Power of Affirmations

Affirmation: *The assertion that something exists or is true.*

—Webster's Universal College Dictionary

THE PROGRAMMING OF your subconscious mind began before you took your first breath.

David B. Chamberlain, editor of *Prenatal Memory and Learning* writes:

> In a famous experiment by Anthony DeCasper and colleagues at the University of North Carolina, Greensboro, mothers read the Dr. Seuss story, "The Cat in the Hat," at regular intervals before birth.
>
> At birth, babies were hooked up to recordings, which they could select by sucking on a non-nutritive nipple. After a few trials, babies cleverly sucked at whatever speed was necessary to obtain their mother's voice reading "The Cat in the Hat".

Similarly, musical passages repeated regularly—such as theme music for the British soap opera "Neighbors" or the bassoon passage from "Peter and the Wolf"—are identified and preferred immediately after birth.

In another experiment, a children's rhyme was repeated each day from week 33 to week 37 of gestation. At the end of this time, still inside the womb, the babies showed memory and learning for this particular rhyme as opposed to similar rhymes they had not heard.

An important message of these diverse findings is that memory and learning seem to be a natural part of being human, including the first nine months in the womb and the years of infancy, defined as the time before speech. Perhaps the biggest surprise is that life in the womb is extremely active and interactive, and that the womb is, in fact, a classroom.

Every moment of our life is filled with constant affirmations of what we perceive to be true or false. How we feel about what we perceive to be true about the world in which we each live is called attitude. Attitude is an emotion. It is how we mentally feel about something.

We affirm thoughts we believe are true or false. "No one loves me! *I will never amount to a hill of beans.* I can't do that! I can't afford that! I can do that! Everyone loves me! I am a good spouse! " We say these things and more to others and to our self. We hear them in our mind as never ending mental chatter. The subconscious acts on affirmations as mental commands.

Repeating your affirmation over and over again is necessary for the process of creating a more positive self-image and for achieving your life goals. The more times you repeat your affirmation, the more effective the subconscious mind is in bringing to fruition that which you affirm. Affirmations program the subconscious mind to do its work. If you don't like the results of how things have turned out for you, listen to what you keep saying to your self.

The Law of Attraction is bringing to us, not the things we should like, or the things we wish for, or the things someone else has, but it brings us 'our own,' the things which we have created by our own thought processes, whether consciously or unconsciously. Unfortunately, many of us are creating these things unconsciously.

—**Charles F. Haanel**

• • •

YOUR MOVE

To affirm the dream, you must define the dream in every detail. Imagine the dream working perfectly before taking the first step toward creating your own affirmation. You must be able to see in your mind's eye the possibilities brought to you by the fulfillment of your dream. Most important, you must believe and have faith it is possible. The inventor visualizes his idea in a similar manner.

Nikola Tesla, one of the greatest inventors of all time. The man who has brought forth the most amazing realities, always visualizes his inventions before attempting to work them out, says, "When I have gone so far as to embody in the invention every possible improvement I can think of, and see no fault anywhere, I put into concrete form the product of my brain. Invariably my device works as I conceived it should; in twenty years there has not been a single exception."

Visualization is a key component in developing affirmations that will improve your self-image and your material status. Learn that you can achieve whatever you *have to have* in life by affirming it as fact and by tapping into the Spirit of the Universe within for guidance. Nothing throughout all of history has ever been achieved without the consent of the mastermind through which the universe was created.

Affirmation 9
I am one with the Spirit of the Universe.
I am not the physical form that I see in the mirror.
I am the observer-self called consciousness.
I am one with the Spirit of the Universe that provides the ultimate in mental capacity and capability. I cannot fail.

I am careful to recognize my negative thoughts, so that even subliminally absorbed, they will not reflect in my self-talk. Thoughts create the words that I say to myself. Those words, though often held secret, are the thoughts that ultimately determine my actions and my destiny. With the Spirit of the Universe as my guide I cannot fail.

15
Affirming Your Dream

If a man would move the world, he must first move himself.

—Socrates, 469-399 B.C

AN AFFIRMATION IS a statement of fact made in faith. When you repeat your written affirmations you are affirming that what you are saying is true and already exist, even before you are actually in possession of that which is affirmed.

When the subconscious accepts your affirmation as fact, it automatically begins the work of making that which you *have to have* come true. Doubt even a little bit and the subconscious will act on that doubt. What you ask for is what you will get.

If you want to lose weight, but you are constantly saying to yourself and others, "I've tried everything and I just can't lose weight," you are affirming a negative statement as though it is fact. In doing so you are programming your subconscious to believe you cannot lose weight. The subconscious mind is not concerned with the outcome; it acts on the words that flow from your thoughts.

You may lose weight on a diet if you follow prescribed actions until you reach your goal. It's much like following a road map to a distant destination or recipe for baking a cake; however, if the mental picture you hold on to is the body you started with, the overweight person you don't want to be, you may not only regain the lost weight, you may even add a few pounds to boot.

When you announce to yourself or others, "I am going to try this new diet. Everyone seems to swear by it," the subconscious files that statement away with emphasis on the word *try* and waits for you to develop a plan you really believe in.

If you want to lose weight or gain weight, you should first change the mental picture of the body that is currently stored in your subconscious mind. Visualize the new body you *have to have*. Believe and affirm the fact as though you already have the body you visualize. If you *have to have* it, the subconscious mind will go to work to make your vision a reality. You might as well start picking out your new wardrobe. What you *have to have* will be achieved through affirmation.

Create a visual tool to help you focus. Find a photograph of a person with the body you *have to have*. Post it on your mirror, dream board or refrigerator. Place the photograph where it is a constant reminder.

Make an affirmation card that reads:

> I *am 125 pounds* (or whatever weight it is that you *have to have*). I am the product of the food I consume. I am consuming only those foods that are nutritional and healthy for me. I am the result of nutritional food and exercise. I am exercising a minimum of twenty minutes every day. I am 125 pounds.
>
> Those two words, I AM, are the magic words that create miracles. If you really believe and you *have to have* it, you will have it.
>
> Seriously think about what you *have to have*. Think about what you are willing to give up to get what you *have to have*.

What action steps are necessary to achieve the results that you *have to have*?

Remember, affirmations without belief and action can lead to stress, depression, anxiety, and a feeling of being a loser.

You should never say to yourself or to anyone else, "I can't" unless that is what you want. In fact, you should remove the words "I can't" from your vocabulary. Refuse to think those words.

If you say, "I can lose weight," what you are actually saying is, "I will sometime in the future" or "I could if I wanted to." "I can or I could," indicates something you can do if you ever get committed to it and *have to have it*. Replace the words "I can" with the words, "I AM," the two most powerful words in any language.

The words "I AM" are so powerful that you must be very careful how you use them. If you say, "I am going to lose weight," that tells the subconscious, "someday." If you say, "I am losing weight," that tells the subconscious, "I am in the process. Haven't lost it yet, but working on it." Remember, an affirmation is affirming what you *have to have* as though you already possess it. I am 125 pounds. (Reread the first paragraph of this chapter.) Be very clear and specific in your request.

Since the subconscious does not know the difference between the truth and a lie, you will need to be very specific about what it is that you *have to have*—what size, what color, how many, how much, when, what you will do, what you are willing to give up to obtain your goal, etc.

• • •

BEING SPECIFIC

Once, long ago, we were enjoying a great country meal at my grandparent's farm. My Uncle J. T. Baker was there having fun with all his nieces and nephews. As usual, he loved to play tricks on us and looked for opportunities to do so.

I wanted to sprinkle some black pepper on my mashed potatoes. The pepper was at J.T.'s end of the table. I said, "J.T. can you pass the pepper." He said, "Yes!"

I waited a few minutes, expecting him to pass the pepper, but he did not.

"J.T., did you hear what I said?" I asked.

"Yes," he responded. But, he still didn't pass the pepper.

I said, "Well, are you going to pass the pepper or not?"

"Oh, I thought you asked if I COULD pass the pepper, which of course I can do, but you did not say, 'please pass the pepper'. There is a difference, you know."

A few minutes later I said, "J.T., please pass the bread."

He said, "Sure! Do you want a whole piece or a half piece?"

I said, "A whole piece, of course."

So, to my surprise, with his finger he punched a hole in the middle of the slice of bread.

On another occasion, while visiting my grandparents, J.T. was once again present. We were sitting at the kitchen table drinking coffee and eating a slice of coconut crème pie. My favorite!

J.T. got up from the table and said, "I'm going to get another cup of coffee. Does anyone want some more."

I said, "Sure! Could you warm my cup up a bit?"

Well, I should have known better. He was gone for what seemed to be a very long time. When he returned he came back with two cups on a tray. I reached for my cup, and when I touched the handle it was scorching hot. It was so hot it burned my fingers. I almost spilled the coffee on the table as I jerked my hand back.

There was no coffee in the cup.

"What is this? Why did you do that?" I yelled, while sucking my burnt fingers.

He said, "Well...it's your fault! I did what you told me to do. You asked me to warm your cup up, so I put it in the oven and warmed it up."

It appears that with some people you cannot win.

From that event and other similar events with my Uncle J.T., I learned to be clearer when I made a request. The lessons J.T. taught me is an example that illustrates how the subconscious works. The subconscious responds to a specific request. If your request is not clear, you might not be happy with the results.

If you want to lose weight, be specific. If you don't have to lose weight, you can think of a thousand reasons why you don't have to. Here is an example of such thinking. "I'm just one of those people who is meant to be a little overweight. It runs in my family. My mother is a large woman. I have big bones. I would weigh less if my bones were smaller. Being a little overweight doesn't bother me, why should it bother you? Diets just don't work for me. I've tried them all, and look at me. I actually gained weight while I was on that diet. Losing weight is just not on my radar right now. Besides, it's in my genes, but I'll figure it out one day. You just wait and see."

In addition to making a specific command, affirmations must be done in present tense. Only *present tense affirmations* have value. The object is to reprogram the subconscious mind. If you use the words that indicate something you plan to do in the future, the subconscious will respond with, "Okay...when you are ready, let me know."

Don't worry about the how to. Don't say to your self, "I am lying to myself. I can't do this!" When you say, "I am lying to myself," the subconscious will act on that command and will not believe the affirmation. You have to decide. Your subconscious mind does not care one-way or the other. It is a matter of working in faith.

As a child I unknowingly affirmed the very thing I did not want. The thoughts *my father hates me, he never listens to me, and he really believes I will never amount to a hill of beans* were not true at all. Fathers naturally love their children, but because of those negative interpretations I believed he hated me and that he wished I had never been born. The negative interpretations led to negative affirmations that I held onto and repeated over and over in my mind. This caused me to question my value as a person and brought to me the very things that I did not want.

• • •

GOOD ADVICE
If your desire is to be wealthy know this: wealthy people tend to do what poor people will not do. If you want to be wealthy, don't emulate the poor, unless your goal is to be poor. Find a successful person you admire and discover what he is doing. Jim Rohn says, "Get an appointment with a rich person, even if you have to pay him for his time. Take him to lunch and pick up the tab. You'll be surprised how excited he will be to share his ideas. Just one good idea could change your life forever."

Anthony Robbins, in his book, *Awaken The Giant Within,* calls emulating other people modeling. He says, "I'll tell you now that the best strategy in almost any case is to find a role-model, someone who's already getting the results you want, and then tap into his knowledge. Learn what they are doing, what their core beliefs are, and how they think. Not only will this make you more effective, it will also save you a huge amount of time because you won't have to reinvent the wheel. You can fine-tune it, reshape it, and perhaps even make it better."

Through your self-talk you've been affirming things in your mind all your life, some positive and some negative. If you think it, believe it, and take action on those things that you affirm as true, you eventually get what you tell your subconscious mind you *have to have.*

> "Whatever the mind can conceive and believe it can achieve."
>
> —**Earl Nightingale**

• • •

CONFESS IT TO POSSESS IT

To possess it you must first have faith and believe that what you cannot see or understand is possible for you. There are many things that you believe, but cannot see. Illusions surround you, yet you believe they exist. For instance, you may be one who believes the illusion that the sun rises in the morning and sets in the evening, but you would be wrong. The sun never rises and it never sets. The earth rotates around the sun and so you perceive a sunrise when the first light from the sun faces your side of the earth. When darkness arrives, you perceive the sun has set. In reality though, it simply means the other side of the earth is facing the sun. The sun never sets and it never rises. The sun is always shining. Therefore, if you believe in sunsets and sunrises, your perception is based on what you have been programmed to believe, that the sun rises and sets.

You can't see the wind, yet you believe it exists because you can see its effect and it can be demonstrated. You can't see the oxygen you breathe; yet you know it exists because you've been taught that without it you would die and that too can be demonstrated. In reality, there are many things that you believe exist that you cannot see, taste, touch, smell or hear.

For the results of your affirmations to become real, you must have faith that what you *have to have*—that thing that you cannot yet touch, taste, smell, hear, and cannot see—will manifest. That is, through faith you speak into existence the things you *have to have*. In this process you must have faith that you will succeed without evidence that you will. To possess it, you must confess it.

> *Thou art snared with the words of thy mouth and thou art taken with the words of thy mouth.*
>
> —Holy Bible - Proverbs 6:2

Affirmation 10

I am the master of my moods, which determines my attitude toward the world.

I am obtaining the results of my thoughts, good and bad; therefore, I will think only positive thoughts.

I am created to achieve a specific preordained purpose. While I will experience difficulty in the ebb and flow of life, I cannot fail.

16
Imagination and the Mind

Imagination is more important than knowledge.

—Albert Einstein

FIRSTHAND EXPERIENCE HAS taught us that self-talk and imagination can activate the power of one's natural instincts. Even while asleep or in a dream-like state, imagination can cause the reptilian brain to act as though danger is imminent, which immediately increases the heart rate and pumps massive amounts of adrenaline into the body. The system automatically goes into survival mode.

• • •

THE DREAM
After getting into bed one night, I couldn't remember if I had locked the backdoor that led from our bedroom to the deck that is connected to the rear of our home. I knew I should have at least checked, but I was very tired and thought I most likely locked it. Since I normally do, I decided not to bother. Surely, I thought, nothing would happen even

if I had left it unlocked. No one had ever tried to break into our home or car. With that, I felt justified to stay in bed.

Just as I was slipping into a very deep sleep, wouldn't you know it, I heard footsteps on the deck coming toward the bedroom door. Slowly the door squeaked open. A very large man stopped in the doorway to look around the room and saw my wife and I in bed asleep. When he was satisfied that we were sound asleep, he slowly closed the door behind him and tiptoed into the bedroom.

My heart began to pound fiercely, almost jumping through my chest. The adrenalin commenced flowing. I was so scared; I was physically paralyzed and frozen to the bed. It felt as though my entire body was chained down and my mouth was filled with cotton. I could not move a muscle and could not have yelled, even as badly as I wanted to.

He was a very large bearded man with long hair. He wore black and white striped overalls with a red plaid shirt and a red baseball cap with the word Indians on the front of it in large white letters. A long hunting knife in a sheath stuck out of his back pocket. He was wearing six-inch work shoes, caked with mud. I remember thinking, oddly enough, that Louise will be awfully mad when she wakes up and finds all that mud on our new carpet.

I thought, "Surprise is what I need. That will be my edge. I'll beat him to a pulp."

"I've got to get rid of the paralysis somehow. God help me… please. Please give me the strength to protect my family," I prayed.

He continued to tiptoe through the bedroom and then into the kitchen, where he stopped at the kitchen sink. Louise was sound asleep and not aware of what was going on. I prayed she would not wake up and scream or do some foolish thing that would let him know we were awake.

The streetlight shining through the kitchen window allowed me to see him standing there. I imagined that he was looking out the window, waiting for someone else to show up. Maybe someone was coming to assist him in the robbery and the murder. "MURDER…oh my goodness," I thought. Suddenly, he turned and began walking back toward our bedroom.

"How can I fight the two of them? If they think they are going to stab us to death, steal whatever they can carry and be on their way, they are mistaken. He's going to get the devil knocked out of him when he comes by my bed. I am not dying without a fight," I thought.

He was about four feet from our bed, passing between the bed and the dresser, on my side of the bed.

Strangely, just at that moment the paralysis left me. I jumped from the bed and hit him in the mouth as hard as I could. I thought I might have broken my hand. I must have cut my knuckles on his front teeth. It was dark, but I was sure my knuckles were bleeding all over the new carpet.

It is strange how I was so concerned with that carpet.

My punch knocked him to his knees, and I quickly grabbed him by the collar, pushed him back and straddled his body. I continued punching him in his face with all my might.

I could see him trying to reach for his hunting knife. I stomped his right arm just below his elbow with my left knee. He let out a yell and began punching me with his left fist under my right rib cage. It hurt so badly, I could hardly breathe. The adrenaline was flowing and the pain drove my anger.

I was thinking as I swung as hard as I could, "This man is not going to go out. I've hit him with everything I've got, but I can't knock him out. I am going to die!"

I continued to hit him with all my strength, which was now waning. "No matter what, I have to win this one, or my wife and children will probably die. I just cannot quit. God help me!"

Our four children were asleep in their bedrooms on the south end of the house. I was not sure they could hear the commotion.

What if he found our children? There is no choice! I have to kill him somehow. I remember thinking, as I began to yell with each punch I threw that at least my family might hear the yells, get out of bed, call the police, or just run. Maybe they would make it if I made enough noise.

I was getting very tired! He knew there was no way I could knock him out. Every muscle in my body screamed for relief and there was not a dry spot on my body.

His body punches were getting the best of me. I was now convinced that I was going to die. I just knew it!

Suddenly the bedroom light came on. My wife screamed, "JOEL...JOEL...WHAT ARE YOU DOING?"

She grabbed my arm and pulled me away from him. I believe the sudden jerking of my arm was what finally woke me from what might have been my most horrible nightmare ever.

There I stood, in my bloody underwear, holding the bleeding fist that I had managed to mangle by beating the top of our dresser to death.

It was so real! I felt I was actually living the nightmare. This is further proof that the subconscious mind, that part of the brain that never sleeps, does not know the difference between what is real and what is not.

Needless to say, I felt extremely foolish while my family looked on at this pathetic creature holding his bleeding hand. I washed up, changed my underwear, cleaned the carpet the best I could, and crawled back into the bed. Unable to sleep, I covered my head to drown out the giggling until early morning.

It was just one of the more terrifying experiences that helped me realize the power of the subconscious mind and the human imagination. I thought to myself, "I may never be the same." And surely, I was not!

You may have had a similar experience or you may know a friend or a relative who has experienced something similar. I have discovered that I am not alone.

I had been subliminally (below conscious level) programmed by my own self-talk and from watching television news casts and sitcoms, reading negative newspaper articles, reports of robberies, murders, drive by shootings, rape, and so forth. The programming took place without my knowledge, but with my total permission. By choosing to read numerous negative articles and by watching scary stories on television, I had developed a deep concern for safety and for survival of my family.

As we read newspapers, magazines, and watch television, we automatically picture what we are reading. It is interesting that we don't think in words, but rather in pictures. And, these pictures remain with us throughout our life. The Chinese learned this long ago and developed their entire language based on pictures rather than an alphabet.

When we say any word such as mountain or automobile, we do not see the word *'mountain'* in our mind, unless we are concentrating on the word itself. Instead we see a generic picture of a mountain. The picture flashes through the mind to our subconscious and back to the conscious mind at nanosecond speed. The speed at which the translation occurs blurs the fact that a picture actually appears in our conscious mind at all.

It is probably fair to say that more information is being handled by the central nervous system (brain) of one's body at any given moment, than in terms of "bits" is being transmitted by the entire United States Telephone system.

—**Leslie H. Hart**

The human brain is powerful and remains mysterious. After all the research that has been done on the human brain, very little is understood.

When we go to sleep at night it is our conscious mind that sleeps. Our subconscious mind continues to do its work, good and bad. It never sleeps. While our conscious mind is in a deep sleep mode, the subconscious mind is dissecting all the days' activities, thoughts and body functions, and is storing the data for later recall. Some scientists are convinced that sleep was created for that purpose—to store, organize, and analyze information in a way that the human mind can recall and use it as needed. When we get ready to use the files stored in our subconscious mind, they are instantly uploaded to our conscious mind, where the conscious mind is able to use them and manipulate them.

Every time an impression is received, the process of receiving, comparing, and storing takes place in a nanosecond. A nanosecond, according to the dictionary, is one billionth of a second. In the metric system and in technical usage, it is one billionth of a specified unit. We cannot blink our eyes that fast.

As Leslie H. Hart says, "To use comparative analysis, the mind must have two or more elements in which to find matches, and to apply differential analysis, two or more in which to find differences. As inputs to the brain number billions of bits per second, these processes minimally involve millions of factors, processed simultaneously along hundreds or thousands of proster hierarchies (proster theory). This is not an operation we can simplify by putting a pigeon in a Skinner box."

Before any action on our part takes place, every conscious thought is compared to data stored in our mental hard drive. It all happens instantly, all-the-while creating our would-be best selling story...our life movie.

The perception of the world in which we experience life is generated by thoughts of the immediate experience combined with thoughts already stored in our subconscious mind. As we gather the experiences, compare the data and write the screenplay for our life movie, we add imaginary events that have become reality to us. We experience life based on what is true and what we imagine to be true about ourselves within context.

Sometimes when we observe our own life's play we are fed incorrect information by sources whose motivation it is to take advantage of us. We are frequently subliminally programmed by local and national events through advertising and various forms of propaganda.

Even the cartoons children watch are filled with subliminal programming with carefully chosen words, actions and scenery.

Likewise, textbook disinformation is stretching our imagination concerning the world we inhabit. Carefully read the words written in schoolbooks your children are required to read. You might learn that your child is being programmed to believe things that are at the very least, highly questionable. Check it out! Unfortunately, the bad stuff remains in their subconscious and it will be there until they die.

Rit Nosotro, in his book *History of Textbook Propaganda,* says: "Textbook propaganda is a tool that has been used since the invention of the printing press by communist dictators and democratic capitalists to mold the thoughts of a child into the goals of the state."

Undesirable programming that is subliminally absorbed is the creative assimilation of word pictures that are embedded in our subconscious in such a way that we begin to believe the pictures are our own thoughts and ideas.

Affirmation 11
I am somebody.
 Today is a new beginning.
 There has never been, nor will there ever be, another person exactly like me.
 I am somebody. I am unique in the universe. I am blessed beyond comprehension.
 I am somebody. The body I occupy is a gift from God. It is the perfect body for God's plan in my life.
 I am somebody. God has blessed me with a powerful brain and mind where genius resides.
 I AM SOMEBODY! I CANNOT FAIL!

17
I Think I Am

*I am not who you think I am. I am not who I think I am.
But, I am who I think you think I am.*

—Thomas Cooley

EVEN WITH EXCELLENT mental capacity and with the ability to analyze and comprehend, we often try to become the person we believe others want us to be. We play the role of this imaginary person as though we are starring in an award-winning movie, and most of the time we do it without even realizing it.

The desire to be loved, to be accepted, and to feel important is often so strong that we will do anything to emulate those people we respect and admire. We believe that being popular and accepted by those we admire justifies our efforts to emulate others. Emulation of others comes from an ego driven subconscious desire to be more than we think we are. The ego always wants more.

Dr. John Dewy, one of America's most profound philosophers, supports this fact. He says, "The deepest urge in human nature is the desire to be important."

We are programmed to believe acceptance is one of the measurements of who we are as a person. If we feel our peers do not accept us, we often imagine we are being falsely profiled and victimized. When we feel we are not included, we have a tendency to feel inferior, and we often don't understand why. No wonder it is so difficult for children to comprehend the reality of who they really are. Most people have no idea of who they really are and so become, "I am who you think I am."

Ego loves to attach itself to things and has no problem attaching to things that provide us with the assurance that somehow we count for something. Ego wants us to believe that we must measure up and become like others we surround ourselves with in order to be accepted and loved.

• • •

OUR CHANGING PHILOSOPHY
What is our current teaching philosophy? How can we instill in our children the knowledge that they are loved, important, and that they are somebody? What are the children of the world being taught?

Viewing the academic education system from the outside it may appear to be cold and non-caring. Visit with a few teachers in open dialogue and you will learn that from their point of view the problem is not about knowing how to teach, what to teach, or knowing what to do. It is not about not caring about the students. The major challenge is about the inability to teach in a system that mandates use of a program that has failed the students and their teachers. It boils down to the system's inability to deliver curriculum too much of the undisciplined student body.

The powers that be—the lawmakers, state boards of education, and the local school boards—those who determine what our students are to be taught and how they are to be taught, make the rules that teachers must follow.

Teachers are required to teach with little variance the curriculum that is provided to them. The laws are written in such a way that puts the student between the home, where guilt-ridden parents provide less and less guidance, and the school system, where the atmosphere for learning and discipline are difficult to administer.

With a crippled education system, it is no wonder that children in most states are dropping below the desired academic performance level, with many dropping out altogether. All too often when children leave the school system, employers are straddled with teaching the basics.

• • •

EDUCATION AND THE WORKPLACE

The challenge to business is that once hired, often the employees have to be re-educated in subjects that they should have learned in school. Many students who graduate from high school come to the marketplace with diplomas that have very little value. If students cannot spell, read, write, add, subtract, or divide, what kind of workforce are we creating? If a student does not know how to make change, how will he or she survive in today's world? Retraining costs have to be recovered and are most often passed on to the customer.

Academic and moral education is vitally important. What we send out into the world comes back to us multiplied and running over. It only requires a little observation to understand that if we don't reach children while they are young, we may lose them completely.

It is pretty obvious the rules of the *setup* are not being properly taught or fully understood and applied. The law of cause and effect says that for *every action there is a reason and a cause*, which creates an equal but opposite reaction. The law is a universal law. It is a law of duality. What goes up must come down. We don't have to pursue the lessons. They occur automatically. Life will teach us! It just happens! We soon get the message, though often harshly.

The law of cause and effect is similar to the boomerang effect. When you throw the boomerang out there, the boomerang comes back. Sometimes you think it has gone and will not come back, but when you least expect it, the boomerang comes back and hits you in the back of the head. The world of education is now throwing the boomerang with the current choice of passing students who do not meet the academic requirements. Before long the boomerang will hit the education system in the backside, having a profound effect on our economic and social system.

The law of cause and effect is given to us in the parable of the sower in the Holy Bible - *Galatians 6:7: Be not deceived; God is not mocked: for whatsoever a man soweth, that shall he also reap*. It also means we will reap more abundantly what we have sown and thus it becomes a self-fulfilling prophecy.

In his book, *The Nature of Personal Premises/Creating Ideal Personal Futures*, J. D. Adams says:

> The well-known term 'self-fulfilling prophecy' (Merton, 1948) suggests that whatever one holds in one's mind, even subconsciously, tends to occur in one's life. In other words, whatever we dwell on expands. If we dwell on problems, we find more problems; if we dwell on happiness, we find more happiness. These premises become self-reinforcing in that the more often one of them 'comes true,' the more absolute it becomes and less subjectable it is to question.

When we feel unloved, unwanted, unimportant, not accepted, and certainly not very popular, we tend to verbalize those feelings to ourselves. In so doing, we harbor the things that eventually become true.

Fortunately, I was raised in a God-fearing East Texas family. I had little doubt about my mother's concern for my education, my future, or her love for me. Even so, I can remember times in my life when I didn't feel loved. There were many times when I felt like a loser. I often felt like I didn't belong.

The following story I share as an example of how the most innocent events can effectively create negative self-talk that can destroy a child's self-image and self-esteem. This is another scene from my *mental movie* that had a dramatic effect on my life.

• • •

AN EDUCATION AT THE SWIMMING HOLE
On a hot, sultry Sunday afternoon in July 1942 my dad, my uncle, and a couple of older cousins were walking down the trail through the pasture that led to the swimming hole in the creek behind our old East Texas farm house. I was six-years-old. I could not swim and was afraid of drowning, but I wanted to watch them swim. Dad told me not to follow them to the creek because I might fall in. The old swimming hole was about twenty feet across and was very deep in the middle.

I was hardheaded and had a tendency not to listen, which got me in trouble more than once. I followed them from a distance. There was a large tree on the creek bank with branches that leaned out over the creek. My Dad had tied a heavy rope around one of the bigger limbs. They loved to swing out over the swimming hole and flip and dive, or drop down into the water.

"Buddy, (my nick name) if you keep following us, when we get to the creek I'm going to throw you in, clothes and all," Dad yelled as he looked back at me. He continued looking back now and then to see if I was still there. Of course, I didn't believe he would throw me in, so I continued to follow them. Bad choice!

When they finally reached the bank, everyone stripped and jumped into the water. Laughing, splashing around, and swinging from the rope, they seemed to be having a great time. I thought to myself, "I wished that I could do that too."

Suddenly Dad disappeared and I wondered where he went. I watched closely, but he was nowhere to be found.

He had swum underwater and snuck up onto the bank on the far end of the swimming hole and hid behind some tall grass where I could not see him. He snuck up on me, scooped me up, and threw me into the water, clothes and all, just as he had promised.

I sank like a rock. My uncle quickly grabbed me and pulled me to the surface. I came up gasping for breath and spitting water. A second longer under water and I might have taken the fatal dose. I was totally petrified.

"See, I told you. You're gonna learn to mind me one of these days," Dad yelled as he jumped back into the swimming hole, grabbed me by the arm and took me to the creek bank. As he put me on the bank he said, "Now git!"

Everyone laughed until their sides hurt as they watched me run back to the house soaking wet and crying my heart out. Mom removed my wet overalls and dried me off. She held me close trying to console me. I felt so much love from my mother and so unloved by my dad.

All the women crowded around and talked about how horrible it was to treat a kid like that. Mom took me by the hand and we walked back down the cow trail to the swimming hole.

There was a lot of yelling and arguing, with threats made to everyone in the swimming hole for what they did to me. I remember how they all were laughing and saying, "Hey, we were just playing. We didn't mean no harm." I'm sure Mom had a few additional words for Dad when he got back home.

My mom's actions made me feel her love for me. She made me feel important and secure.

From that day forward, through that experience, I felt totally unloved by my Dad. I truly believed he wished I had never been born. That experience is one of my self-imposed stories that I kept hidden in the back of my mental closet all my life. It remained hidden in my subconscious until I finally realized it was totally false.

Oh, he through me in the creek alright, but he did not do it to hurt me and he did not do it because he hated me. He was simply trying to teach me a valuable lesson in life; to respect my mother and father. It was a lesson I have never forgotten. It was only a story based on my perception and interpretation of those events; an interpretation that I had convinced myself was true; that my dad did not love me.

Here is another episode that illustrates self-fulfilling prophecies. Below is my interpretation of what I perceived to be true at the time.

• • •

THE CAT'S MEOW

We were a poor family living in the East Texas countryside in an old run-down farmhouse that was provided to us as part of my dad's sharecropper agreement. There was no running water, nor electricity and one rundown outhouse. It was 1942, and to say the least, it was about as rural in the true since of the word as one could get. It was a normal life style for a sharecropper's family in those days. As a small child I had not experienced any other life style. I did not know we were poor. It seemed to me everyone lived the same in those days.

Nature was our playground. A smorgasbord of beautiful wild flowers filled the green pasture with nature's color pallet of green, yellow, brown, red, and lilac. A quiet breeze blew making the grass and flowers move like ocean waves. What a beautiful summer day God had given us to romp and play. My big sister, Shirley, was about nine-years-old and I was about six.

Shirley's cat had just given birth to a litter of five kittens, whose eyes were barely open.

"Let's take the kittens out in the pasture and play," Shirley said. She put the kittens inside a cardboard box she had found. I followed her up the path, dragging an old homemade quilt Mom loaned us to spread on the grass.

Mamma cat followed behind, chasing the blanket, trying to jump on it now and then as we hurried to what Shirley believed was the best place in the pasture to spread the quilt. It was a happy day, and I felt safe and loved by my big sister.

"Buddy, help me spread the blanket," she said as she sat the box down on the grass.

The kittens were crying for their mother and were trying to climb the walls of the box, while mother cat stood with her paws on the edge of the box peering in. She seemed to be saying, "Mamma's here! Everything will be alright."

Although the grass was tall and the breeze blew in gusts now and then, we finally got the blanket spread. Shirley set the box in the middle of the blanket and we sat facing each other on the edges of the blanket in our attempt to keep the wind from blowing the blanket off the grass.

Shirley took the kittens out of the box, and I tried to help. "Buddy, watch out. Don't hold it so tight, you'll squash it."

The kittens were trying to walk on the blanket, but were having difficulty because the blanket could not lie flat on the ground. They would walk a few steps and roll over. I thought it was funny and so did Shirley. They were rolling and bumping into each other. I was jumping up and down on my knees with excitement.

Suddenly we heard one of the kittens squeal. Shirley looked around to see where the squeal came from and noticed one of the kittens was missing. Mamma cat was peeking under the blanket.

"Get up, Buddy!" I just sat there, not understanding.

"Why?"

"Get up," she screamed. "I think one of the kittens is under the blanket."

She quickly picked up all the kittens and gently placed them back into the box, and together we lifted the blanket. There it was...dead as a mackerel!

"You killed it! You squashed my kitten! You killed my kitten! You're a killer! You are going to hell! Don't you know...thou shalt not kill? What kind of person are you? My brother, a killer! What are we going to do now? God will never forgive you for this," she screamed.

I did not know what to say. I stood there in total shock. I went from total happiness to total shock in less than a heartbeat. I knew it was true. The Bible plainly says so, according to Mom, "Thou shalt not kill."

My mind was suddenly fried. "Boy, I have done it now," I thought. "I am doomed to hell and there's nothing anyone can do about it, especially me. I am going get my rear end spanked to a pulp for killing that kitten."

I didn't know where to turn, or how I was going to prevent it. My mother was a firm believer in not sparing the rod, nor spoiling the child. My mind was rapidly filling with negative self-talk.

When I got in trouble and needed a spanking, she often made me go out to the willow tree in the back yard and pick a switch. Somehow, no matter how small the switch, she could whip me half to death with it. I learned that she would not hit me as hard with a large switch. All this was running through my mind as we hurried back to the house to break the news to Mom. I was sure Shirley would love to watch me die. It would have made her day.

While I was dragging the quilt and following mamma cat, Shirley was crying and screaming, "Killer, killer! You are a murderer. You are going to hell. I can't believe you killed it. Mamma, Mamma, Buddy is a killer," she yelled.

I ran after her, crying and yelling, "I didn't mean to do it. I'm sorry! What can I do? I didn't mean to." Knowing full well God was going get me for this one, I just wanted to disappear somewhere, somehow.

Shirley ran into the house yelling, "Mamma, Mamma, you won't believe it. Buddy is a murderer. He killed one of my kittens. He's going to go to hell, Momma. He's a killer."

"Let me see!" Mom said, as she looked in the box.

"What happened?"

As I look back on that day I realize now, I had embellished what I perceived to be the truth concerning that event. I imagined Shirley, with eyes full of tears and slobbering from both sides of her mouth and exuberating the hatred she must have felt for me at that moment. She told her gruesome side of the story of how I jumped up and down and was trying to squash that kitten on purpose.

"Hush, Shirley! What happened, Buddy?" Mom said.

"I don't know. I thought they were all on the quilt. I didn't see one get under it. I don't know how it got there. I didn't put it there. Mom, Shirley said I'm a murderer and I'm going to hell. Mamma, I don't want to go to hell."

"You are! You are going to hell. You're a killer," Shirley declared.

"Dry it up, Shirley! No, you are not going to go to hell. God is a very forgiving God. You didn't really do that on purpose, did you?"

"No, Mam! No! I didn't!"

"Well, God loves us with all His heart and He loves you, especially right now. All you have to do is ask God to forgive you for accidentally killing one of His kittens and He will forgive you. Everything will be all right. The little kitten is now with Jesus," she said as she put her loving arms around me.

Momma prayed and asked God to forgive me. Shirley was looking at me, one eye open, with a snarled look on her face. No doubt she was thinking that she wished I would drop dead on the spot.

I felt loved by my mother. I felt betrayed and unloved by my big sister.

Surely, we had a funeral for the dead kitten. I cannot recall.

To this day I have trouble killing a roach without remembering that episode in my life. Thou shalt not kill. I know with all my heart that I have been forgiven and I will not go to hell for killing that kitten.

It took me a long time to forgive my dad for throwing me in the creek and my sister for accusing me of murdering her cat, but the following event almost destroyed all hope for me. This life event threw my mind into a fog, destroyed my self-esteem, and created a world so full of doubt about life in general and especially about other human beings. It had me wishing I had never been born. Surely, I would *never amount to a hill of beans* or anything else, as far as I could visualize at that time in my life.

• • •

THE MISSING QUARTER

Bonner Elementary was a two-story brick building on the northeast side of the city. I was in the second grade. It was a cold November day in 1944.

We were on the playground for our regular ten o'clock recess. I had forgotten my jacket, which was in the classroom clothes closet. It was much colder outdoors than I thought it would be, and we still had twenty minutes before recess was over.

Mrs. Clark was my teacher. She was about twenty-eight years old, very nice, and beautiful. I remember that in writing class if we held our hand in just the right position, she would give us a piece of candy. I was in love with her.

"Mrs. Clark, may I go get my coat? I'm really cold," I asked.

"Sure! Just be sure you turn out the lights and close the classroom door and come right back."

I ran up the hill as fast as I could to our classroom on the second floor, opened the closet door and took my coat off the hanger. I turned out the lights and closed both the closet door and the classroom door behind me, just as Mrs. Clark had asked me to do.

Putting on my coat, I ran back to the playground so I would have time to pester my favorite girl, Viola. Of course, Viola could have cared less. Every boy in school was in love with Viola. She was very popular, and I thought she was the prettiest girl in the whole school.

We returned to our classroom and around 11:45 we lined up in the hallway for our walk to the cafeteria. I don't remember what was discussed during class after we returned. I was thinking about Viola and daydreaming about what I was going to do when I got home from school.

We slowly made our way to the cafeteria, most of us carrying brown bag lunches. As we often traded meals, I wondered who I could swap lunch with. On a good day my lunch might be deviled ham, tuna fish, or peanut butter and jelly. At the end of the month my lunch was often mayonnaise and sugar between two slices of white bread, which was not an uncommon lunch for a lot of children in those days.

As I think back on those days, mayonnaise and sugar sandwiches weren't all that bad. Although I resist, I have a strong urge to eat one every now and then.

We were almost inside the cafeteria when Mrs. Clark tapped me on the shoulder and said, "Joel, I need to see for a moment, privately."

As you might recall, when the teacher asked to see you privately, it usually meant trouble or something had happened at home. I was bewildered, scared, and not sure what had happened.

"Joel, Sarah is missing her lunch money. You were the only one in the room during recess. We are wondering if you found the money on the floor and picked it up when you got your coat. She said she put the quarter in her desk right before we went out for recess. When she came back it was gone."

Most people on our side of town were fairly poor in those days. I've always believed Sarah may have lied because she was too embarrassed to admit she didn't have lunch money. Maybe she thought the teacher would feel sorry for her and give her a free lunch.

Most all the children walked to school or rode their bikes in those days. Maybe she had spent it on the way to school at the local independent grocery store for candy or something. I don't really know, but I do know I didn't take her quarter.

"If you have the money I would appreciate your returning it now. If you don't give it to me, I'll have to take you to the principal's office," Mrs. Clark said.

I said, "I didn't take her money. I just got my coat and came back to the playground like you told me to do."

"Maybe we better go talk to Mr. Cox. Come with me."

I felt so unloved by Mrs. Clark.

For corporal punishment, which was allowed in those days, Mr. Cox used a wooden paddle with holes in it. Occasionally he used a red rubber heater hose. Everyone knew about the paddle and the heater hose and how he seemed to love divvying out the licks. The handwriting was on the wall for me. Not a good thing for a boy with a low tolerance for pain.

Something told me I was not going to be able to convince them I was innocent. The circumstantial evidence was stacked against me. Mom always said, "Troubles come in bunches like bananas." She was right, a mayonnaise and sugar sandwich and now this. I imagined my classmates eating and talking about me in the cafeteria.

The library was empty, except for nine six-foot reading tables with three chairs on each side, along with books that filled shelves around the room. There were four very tall windows with beige canvas shades. The upper and lower sections of the windows were partially cracked opened for ventilation. The playground was right outside those windows

"Find a chair and stay there until I get back," Mrs. Clark said in a disgusted tone as she pulled down the shades.

I was not born in a turnip patch. I knew when she closed those shades that meant she was convinced that I had taken Sarah's quarter. Of course, that meant serious trouble for me.

"Yes'um! What are you going to do?" I asked trying to hide my fear.

"I'm going to get Mr. Cox. He'll want to talk to you about this."

"Yeah...right! Talk...I'll bet!" I thought.

The door opened wide as the little shrimp of a man walked in. His 5 ft. 8 in., 170 lb. potbellied frame, was clad in a gray double breasted and pinstripe suit. The lenses of his glasses were thick and round. The frames of his glasses made his eyes appear even more beaded than they were. His hair was combed straight back and parted in the middle. I still feel a bit of anger as I recall this event. I will have to spend more time compressing this event. The picture of him in my mind is as clear as though it were yesterday.

Having once admired Mr. Cox I believed him to be a good man. It is amazing how events can change one's perception of things. My new opinion of him was he was a small in statue and small in mind

If that man smiled, his face would have cracked for sure. It is amazing that he ever became a principal. The person responsible for putting him in that position must have been missing a few bricks. Either that or the school system was extremely short of talent in those days.

"Okay," he said. "You can make it easy on yourself or you can make it hard. It's all up to you. We know you took the money, so don't try to deny it. Just tell us you took it, return the money and everything will be all right. We won't even tell your parents. Just hand over the money, and we'll forget the whole thing."

"Liar...liar, pants on fire," I remember thinking.

"I don't have any money, and I didn't take any money. Somebody else must have done it. I didn't take it," I said, as I pleaded my case.

"Son, there is one thing I can't stand and that is a liar. We know for sure you've got the money, so hand it over," he said sternly.

"You are wrong. I didn't do it. I don't have the money. You can search me," I shouted back.

They searched every inch of my body. Afterwards they stood looking at each other for a few seconds.

"We don't know what you did with it, but we know no one else could have taken the money. It had to be you. Now, we are not going to leave this room until you tell us you took the money and show us where it is," he said, smirking.

"We know you took it," Mrs. Clark said.

"I did not take the money," I responded in anger.

"Yes, you did."

"No, Ma'am, I didn't."

"Yes, you did. We know you did. Now...just own up to it!"

The drilling continued. "Yes, you did!" "No, I didn't!" I began to cry.

Although the interrogation only lasted about thirty minutes or so, it seemed to last for hours. Being only eight years old, I didn't know what to do. I knew I was innocent.

Finally, I came up with this hair-brained idea of confessing to a crime that I didn't commit. I would tell them I lost the money and I would go home and get some money out of my piggy bank to repay the stolen money. That way I could go home, tell my Mom, and get her to help me even though she would be outraged by the very thought that someone was accusing her boy of theft. She would call my dad and they would come back to school with me, and my dad would beat this little shrimp to a pulp.

By this time, I was having mental convulsions. What if this didn't work? My dad had always told me never to admit to something I didn't do. "If someone accuses you of something you did not do, always stand firm. If you did something you are accused of, you have to admit the truth. You've got to be a man!" He evidently never had little Hitler and the prune face Clark (not so beautiful anymore) on his case. Nonetheless, I decided it was my only chance, so I went for it.

"Okay! Okay! I did it! I found the quarter on the floor, but I lost it in the sand on the playground. I tried to find it, but I couldn't. I have some money in my piggy bank. Let me go home and I will bring a quarter back for her."

I lied! I had no money in a piggy bank. I didn't even have a piggy bank.

Cox grinned and looked at prune face.

"Just what I thought! You know you're going to get some licks for this, don't you?" he said with a smirk on his face.

"No, Sir! You said if I gave the money back you would just forget about it."

"Mrs. Clark, if you will stay here with Joel I'll get the paddle. You will receive three licks. Normally you would receive many more, but because you are now telling us the truth, I am reducing your punishment. We will, however, expect you to go home this afternoon, get the money, and return with it in the morning. If you don't, you will receive five additional licks when you return to school tomorrow," he said smugly as he stood in the library doorway.

I felt diarrhea coming on. The hate for these two people boiling up in my mind, coupled with the fear of the famous paddle, was almost too much.

"If Mr. Cox hurts me, my Daddy is gonna be real mad about this," I said to Mrs. Clark.

"And he should be. I'd be mad too if I found out my son was stealing someone's lunch money," she said.

I could tell she was not too swift. She had missed the whole point of my statement, but no doubt she would eventually discover what I was saying at some point later during the week. I had seen my daddy's temper demonstrated many times.

The big man returned to the room with the paddle dangling from a strip of leather attached to the paddle and hung around his right wrist. He swung it up to his hand and slapped it against his left palm several times just to give emphasis to what I was about to receive.

"Bend over and hold on to the chair. Now, do you understand why I'm doing this?"

"No, Sir! You told me you would forget it if I told you I got the money. Why are you doing this to me? You know my dad ain't gonna like this. You're gonna be real sorry. You just wait."

"Your dad will understand, just as I would understand if a principal had to correct my son. And if you keep smart mouthing me, I'm going to give you more licks. Do you understand that?"

As I bent over the chair, I thought to myself, "Easy for him to say! He doesn't even have a son. If he knew my dad, he'd think a long time before he hit me with that thing."

WHACK! I grit my teeth trying to hold the tears back. WHACK! This time harder! I yelled, "STOP, you're hurting me." WHACK, came the third lick. All I could think about then was, "Thank God it's over."

"Go wash your face and come to my office when you're finished," he said.

I could barely walk. Standing on my tiptoes and looking in the bathroom mirror, I tried hard to see the damage he had done, but the mirror was too high. I pulled down my jeans and managed to see a couple of red welts. "He bruised me," I thought. "Mom and Dad ain't gonna like this for sure."

I returned to Mr. Cox's office and sat down in the chair in front of his desk. Tears were flowing as I tried real hard to be brave.

I had a crazy thought, "Wonder if he has books stacked in his seat to make him appear taller. One of these days, when I get big, I'm gonna come back here with a paddle and make him take his pants down. I'm gonna whip his butt 'til the sun don't shine. You can count on it. He's gonna get his."

"Joel, it hurt me more than it did you to have to administer those licks."

"Good grief!" I wondered! "Where did he get that idea?"

However, we cannot tolerate thievery in this school from anyone. If I had a son who had done what you did, he would be treated the same. Now go home and don't forget to bring the quarter back with you in the morning."

"Yes, Sir," I said, thinking how much I was going to love seeing his face when my dad got hold of him. I had never experienced this much anger in my entire short life.

I ran most of the way back home, which was only a mile or so. The entire time I wondered how my parents were going to take all this.

Mom was ironing when I arrived home. "Well, my goodness, what brings you home so early?" She asked as she laid the iron on its end on the ironing board.

"Mom, you won't believe what happened to me at school. They said I stole a quarter from Sarah, a girl in my class. I'm supposed to come home, get a quarter, and take it back to school with me in the morning. Mr. Cox gave me three licks with a paddle, but I didn't do anything. I did not take that girl's quarter, Mamma. It hurt," I said hurriedly, sniffling and pulling down my pants to show her the marks.

"Whoa! Wait just a minute! Are you telling me you told Mr. Cox you stole a quarter from a little girl in your class?" She asked as she grabbed my arm.

"I didn't steal any money, Mamma. But I had to tell 'am I did, so I could come home and get you. They wouldn't let me alone. I had to!"

"You mean you lied to them, and told them you got it?"

"Yes, Ma'am! I had to! They said if I just told them I took the money they wouldn't do anything, but they whipped me anyway."

"We're going back to that school and get this mess straightened out right now. If I find out you stole that quarter, your bottom ain't gonna hold shucks. You know that, don't you? You're telling me for sure, you didn't get that quarter?"

"Yes, Ma'am! I'm telling you I did not get that quarter. I don't know who did, but it wasn't me, I promise. You know I wouldn't lie to you, Mamma," I said as I pleaded my case.

"You know how your dad feels about fessing up to something you didn't do. I don't know how I'm gonna keep him off your back, Buddy."

Mom pulled her apron off and we headed for the door. Just as we reached the front porch Uncle Robert, Mom's brother-in-law, pulled up into the driveway in his old black step-side pickup Ford truck. He got out of the truck and started walking toward the house.

"Where are ya'll going?" he asked.

"Robert, can you take us to Buddy's school? He's in trouble, and I need to get this stuff straightened out right now," she said.

"Sure, let's go. What happened?" Robert asked in the same breath.

"I'll tell you on the way," Mom responded.

She told him what I had told her. Uncle Robert became very angry. I had never seen him so mad. "What is yore principal's name, Boy?" he asked angrily.

Uncle Robert was uneducated academically, but was well versed in the ways of the world. In addition, he was a strict disciplinarian, maybe even more so than my own father. He was a thin scrappy man about five-feet ten and was not afraid of anything or anybody.

He always called me 'boy' for some reason. I guess he couldn't remember either one of my names. He called his wife 'woman' and she didn't seem to mind. Although he only reached the few grades in school, he was an honest, hard-working farmer, and he tried his best to live by Biblical laws as he understood them.

"Mr. Cox," I said.

"What's yore teacher's name?" he demanded.

"Mrs. Clark!"

"Boy, are ya for shore you're telling the truth?" he asked in his slow East Texas country drawl.

"Yes, Sir! I promise."

"Okay! I believe you. You ain't never given me no reason to believe you are a liar. Stretch the truth a bit, but you ain't never lied to me. When we get thar, you jest be quiet. We're gonna handle this thang," he said firmly.

He had been selling his vegetables at the wagon yard, a farmer's market downtown Tyler and, as always, Uncle Robert was stopping by to say hello before he returned to his farm just outside of Teaselville.

We pulled up in front of the school, parked the truck, got out, and walked straight to the principal's office. Uncle Robert told Mr. Cox, "Get that dadburn Mrs. Clark, Joel's teacher in here right now."

I never heard such yelling and screaming between adults before. There was some bad stuff going on behind those closed doors that day. As I waited in the outer waiting room, I was smiling on the inside and praying everything was going to be okay. "They sure messed with the wrong boy when they messed with me," I thought.

I had no idea what Uncle Robert and Mom were doing, but whatever it was, it was not going good for Mr. Cox and Mrs. Clark. I heard Uncle Robert say, "You got proof? You better dang well have some proof! I want to see it right now."

After what seemed to be a very long time, things got a little quieter. Finally they all came out of Mr. Cox's office. Mr. Cox and Mrs. Clark with red faces, obviously embarrassed, walked over to me.

Mr. Cox spoke first, "It looks like we owe you an apology. We don't have any proof you took anything. We're sorry for putting you through all this. I am especially sorry for spanking you. I should have asked your Mom and Dad to be with us. Maybe things would have been different. I don't know, but I'm sorry."

"Me too! I mean, I'm sorry too," Mrs. Clark said, rubbing her eyes with her handkerchief. It looks like I jumped the gun. Can you forgive me?"

I wanted to tell them both just what I thought of them, but a young man with manners was not supposed to use the language I had in mind. Even though I was positive I could never forgive them, I nodded my head to the affirmative. "Dad wouldn't like that either," I thought.

"It is going to be a cold day in Podunk before I get over this. How am I going to face them and all my friends everyday?" I thought.

Mom had always told me when someone apologizes we should accept it and forgive him. Deep inside though, I hated their guts and hoped bad things would happen to them.

"You go back home with your uncle and your mom. We'll see you tomorrow. The other kids will never know anything about this," Mr. Cox said.

"I know that's right," I thought to myself. "I guarantee it's all over the school by now. Everyone thinks I'm a thief."

I secretly wished Uncle Robert had popped him in the nose. I was really proud of Uncle Robert and Mom. At that moment I believed they really loved me.

For the rest of the day I worried about what my dad was going to do. He was hotheaded. There was just no telling what he would do when he arrived home and got the full story.

My dad had been discharged from the Navy's CBs just a few months prior and was now working for the city fire department as a fireman. He worked twenty-four hours on and twenty-four hours off. I wished it were his twenty-four hours on. He was going to give me a licking and I knew it. I was on the front porch with my head hanging down when he drove up.

Mom and Uncle Robert told him the story and tried to convince him I had to do what I had to do to come home and get them, but it was no use. He could not stand the thought of me admitting to something I didn't do. To him it was the same as if I had done it. I would be guilty in the eyes of everyone at school and all his friends. There would always be that little question mark of whether I really did it or not.

He grabbed me by the arm and jerked me to my feet. Dragging me to the back bedroom while pulling off his belt, he said, "I would have died first. You got that? I would have died first."

He then hit me across my bottom and he kept hitting me. I don't know how many times. He was yelling at me, and hitting me simultaneously. My mind just went numb about the same time that my rear end did.

Suddenly, he stopped. "Do you know why I whipped you? Well, do you?" he yelled, while I was trying to catch my breath.

"Yes, Sir!"

"If I ever hear of you doing something like this again, I'll…" Without finishing the sentence, he stormed out of the room slamming the door behind him and drove off. He didn't speak to anyone. He just slammed the door and left. I don't know for sure where he went, but he didn't come home for a long time.

That night, sleeping was out of the question. I had been spanked to a pulp…twice in the same day. To say I felt used, abused, and unwanted would be the understatement of the century. However, I did make one promise to myself. Never again would I admit to doing something I didn't do. It was a lesson well learned. I felt so unloved by my dad.

Nothing more was ever said about that event. I did notice one thing though, Mr. Cox was not at school for several days for some reason. Maybe that episode made him sick, knowing he had done the wrong thing and all. Maybe he was on vacation. I don't know. In my imagination, I preferred to believe my dad acted on my behalf.

It may have been my imagination, but my classmates seemed to keep their distance. When it came time to choose sides for baseball, soccer, or basketball, I was often the last chosen. I felt alone, as though I had no friends at all.

Looking back, I often believed that because I was the oldest boy, Dad took some of his personal frustrations out on me. He had a very hard childhood. His dad was a very strong disciplinarian, and his grandfather was also.

As I reached adulthood, I wondered if the episodes that happened to him on the Pacific Islands during his short time in World War ll had anything to do with it. I'll never know.

Dad passed away at the age of seventy-eight from congestive heart failure. Although I wanted to ask him about those episodes in his life, I never did. I've often wondered why I was the only child in the room when he took his last breath, but now I know that too was preordained to happen.

Was I an abused child? I don't believe I was. In most families, spanking a child was a common form of punishment in those days.

Many stories, such as these, played a big role in programming me to believe no one loved me and that I had zero personal worth. I even occasionally wondered if my mom really loved me. I can't believe I doubted her love, but at times I did. I knew for sure, at least in my mind, my Dad didn't give a hoot about me. I held those feelings most of my life.

After discussing these events with my sister, Shirley, she had an entirely different perception and interpretation of these events, including different locations, times, ages, weather, confrontations, and outcomes. According to her memories of those events, though they did happen, nothing that I said above happened in just that way. I had created those stories in my own mind. She still believes her perception and interpretation of those events are more in sync with what really happened than my own. And so it goes!

Maybe you have had some similar experiences that you haven't come to grips with—personal emotional issues that you need to let go of; negative experiences you need to compress; feelings of anger that have built up inside your mind; feelings that you have kept hidden in your subconscious; feelings that are causing you to take negative action in your daily life without being consciously aware of them. There are millions of people who feel lost, depressed, and seemingly angry at the world, all because of some event in their past that they have not yet acknowledged or dealt with.

Yesterday is just a memory. We cannot change it no matter how hard we try. We can get negative programming out of our system by facing it, compressing it, and getting on with the business of living a happy and productive life.

We should accept the fact that we are unique individuals. Spirit beings, experiencing life in a physical form. No matter how hard we wish to be, we can never be like 'one of them'.

Affirmation 12
I am a Spirit being designed and created to fulfill a specific purpose in the universe.

I am one with all my brother's and sister's, each of whom have been designed and created to fulfill their specific purpose in the universe.

I am a living spirit, one with God, not a specific race, religious denomination or sect.

I am forever joined together with all creation to serve the purpose of the one God, the Holy Spirit of the Universe.

I cannot fail.

18
A View in the Mirror

In the mirror is a reflection to view,
a form of flesh and bone you think is you.
Hidden in this form that you cannot see,
is your Spirit Being observing me.

—Joel D. Johnson

THE REFLECTION IN the mirror that ego calls "my body," is the form that most people associate with "I", "me" and "myself". Since birth we've been programmed to believe "my body" is the whole person that we are. Ego wants to attach itself to people, places, and things, and so it has attached itself to our body and ego has convinced us that we are the form, the body, we see in the mirror.

The body and brain are physical machines provided to serve our preordained life purpose. The body and brain are specifically designed to serve our purpose for being.

Contrary to what we may believe, although we have a body, we are not our body. Once you realize you are a Spirit being occupying a temporary form, it is possible for you to see others in the same way. You will begin to realize you are one with all creatures in the universe.

We are brothers and sisters in creation, designed for a specific purpose to serve the one God, the Holy Spirit of the Universe.

Newly enlightened, you will begin to love and respect others in a whole new dimension. Though at first, it will not be easy, eventually you will learn to look past the physical form and recognize the kindred spirit of those around you. When you finally let go of ego's illusion, you will begin to grasp what it means to be truly alive.

To find life's truths we must look beyond ourselves, our bodies and we will find life's true discoveries.

—Albert Einstein

• • •

TRANSFORMATION

Transformation begins when you realize the false self-image that you have held on to your whole life is not who you really are.

In his book *Psycho Cybernetics*, Maxwell Maltz, M.D., F.I.C.S, says:

> Whether we realize it or not, each of us carries a mental blueprint or picture of ourselves. It may be vague and ill defined to our conscious gaze. In fact, it may not be consciously recognizable at all. But it is there, complete down to the last detail. This self-image is our own conception of the 'sort of person I am.' It has been built up from our own *beliefs* about ourselves. But most of these beliefs have been formed from our past experiences, our successes and our failures and the way people have reacted to us. Once an idea or belief about ourselves goes into this picture it becomes 'true,' as far as we personally are concerned. We do not question its validity, but proceed to act upon it *just as if it were true.*

• • •

MIND-TO-MIND

I can't remember a day that I didn't have at least one mind-to-mind conversation on the phone, by email, or through texting with someone—often someone who I have never met in person.

Through these mind-to-mind conversations where normal visual body language is absent, we develop a mental picture of the person's personality and what he/she looks like.

In our mind we imagine body language through the ebb and flow of voice projection. Whether we realize it or not, we imagine the person's facial expression as we listen to his/her reaction to our questions. In doing so, we instantly develop a mental picture of the whole person. When we finally meet this person, he/she seldom looks or acts anything like the person we imagined he/she to be. In our own mind we create false images or mental book covers, without having full access to full content.

• • •

JUDGING THE COVER

As I watched my wife reading the paper one morning, I asked, "Do you read every article in the paper?"

"No, I don't. I only read the articles that interest me."

"How do you know which ones interest you if you don't read them?"

"Oh, I can tell by the headline. If it sounds interesting, I read it. If not, I don't."

"Would that apply to books and magazines?"

"Sure. Why not?"

"So, if you were not exposed to TV, radio, and internet advertising concerning certain books or magazines, and you happen to be in a book store and were exposed to various covers, do you believe the books and magazines with the most interesting covers and best titles get chosen more often?"

Her answer, "I would say ninety percent of the time, yes!"

Being captured by the headlines is just human nature. Sometimes we make a quick assessment of people similar to the way we judge articles and books. We just look on the outside and if they interest us we might want to get more information.

Obviously, it's not the outside that counts, but we make our judgments based on the cover anyway. It's human nature, and besides, we've been programmed to do it. We know it's wrong and yet we do it anyway. Let's see…what is that called?

You are unique, powerful, and intelligent. You can accomplish anything. Don't judge yourself by its cover. Seek self-acceptance through understanding and realizing that you are not the reflection in the mirror. You are special. You are the child of the living creator of all things. You are designed for tremendous success.

Affirmation 13
I am living my life as if today is my last day. I will not waste time worrying about failures of yesterday or stress out over a non-existing future. I am alive in the moment. There is no other time.

I am living my life as if today is my last day; therefore, I will cherish each moment of this day, for it will never return.

Today I must tell my loved ones "I love you" because tomorrow is not promised.

I am living my life as if today is my last day. I will not procrastinate. I will not put things off another moment, for this is all there is. I take the challenge and complete the course today.

I am living this day with full confidence and knowing that the actions I take are fulfilling my preordained purpose.

I am living my life as if today is my last day and if it is my last day, I will know that my preordained purpose at this time and place has been fulfilled according to the will of God.

I cannot fail.

19
Self-Acceptance

No real success or genuine happiness is possible until a person gains some degree of self-acceptance.

—**Maxwell Maltz**

SELF-ACCEPTANCE MEANS UNDERSTANDING, accepting, and coming to terms with the person you are right now. Maxwell Maltz, author of *Psycho-Cybernetics*, says:

> Self-acceptance is much easier if you understand that these faults, weaknesses, shortcomings, strengths, and physical attributes belong to you, but they are not you. Many people shy away from healthy self-acceptance because they insist upon identifying themselves with their mistakes. You may have made lots of mistakes, but this does not mean that you are a mistake. You may have challenges expressing yourself properly and fully, but this does not mean you are somehow no good.

The words you say to yourself about being no good and feeling that you should never have been born show up in your character and in your personality. This is how others see you. A person's unique individual characteristics, when acted out, become the world's view of who you are perceived to be.

Webster's dictionary describes personality as the set of emotional qualities and ways of behaving that makes a person different from other people.

Various individual characteristics are learned over a lifetime and become habits stored in your subconscious databank. These learned characteristics can have similarities to another person, yet are unique to you because they are the projection of your life's experiences. In reality, no one else can duplicate such qualities, not even an identical twin. You are not a mistake.

As great as it is to have a good personality, you must realize that you are not your personality. Your personality is something you have. It is not who you are. You have arms and legs and a brain, but you are none of those.

Michael Brown, author of *The Presence Process,* makes this observation:

> From birth we are taught that our identity is that which makes us different from everybody else. In other words, we are taught to believe that our real identity is based on our appearance, our behavior, and our individual life circumstances. Therefore, we mistakenly believe that we are our body, the sum of our behaviors, and the circumstances that we are experiencing. Yet, these outer attributes simply constitute passing experiences that we are having; they do not and cannot tell us who and what we really are.

Self-acceptance is realizing that although your body is flesh and bone, the authentic self that is living within the body is a spirit being. You are one with God, He in you and you in Him. When you recognize the authentic self, ego disappears and the influence of programmed weaknesses have less control over your life, allowing you to be and feel the authentic person that is real inside you.

God is not a person of flesh and bone. He is an omnipresent spirit alive in all things. He knows you extremely well and He knows all the secrets you have hidden away in your mental closet. He is even aware of the secrets that you are not consciously aware of. He knows when you make mistakes, how you made those mistakes, and why you made those mistakes. He is one within you and you are in Him. You cannot hide. No matter how hard you try to disappoint Him, He loves you anyway. He already knows your final outcome.

Eckhart Tolle, author of *The Power of Now*, elaborates on this concept:

> What you perceive as a dense physical structure called the body, which is subject to disease, old age, and death, is not ultimately real. It is not you. It is a misperception of your essential reality that is beyond birth, and death, and is due to the limitations of your mind, which, having lost touch with Being, creates the body as evidence of its illusory belief in separation and to justify its state of fear. But do not turn away from the body, for within the symbol of impermanence, limitation, and death that you perceive as the illusory creation of your mind is concealed the splendor of your essential and immortal reality. Do not turn your attention elsewhere in your search for the truth, for it is nowhere else to be found but within our body.
>
> Do not fight against the body, for in doing so you are fighting against your own reality. The body that you can see and touch is only a thin illusory veil. Underneath it lies the invisible inner body, the doorway into Being, into life unmanifested. Through the inner body, you are inseparably connected to this Unmanifested One Life, birthless, deathless, and eternally present. Through the inner body, you are forever one with God.

• • •

CONSCIOUSNESS

To the individual who calls himself a realist, the world in which he lives is mostly a matter of perception. He perceives his own reality as being absolute. He perceives reality through the mirror, a visual sense of being.

As you look at the body in the mirror, with all its weaknesses, blemishes, and other physical attributes, who is the observer? Who is it that is experiencing the act of looking into the mirror? You are! And who are you? You are a spirit being, conscious energy. And what is consciousness?

In his book, *A New Earth, Awakening to Your Life's Purpose,* Eckhart Tolle further explains:

> Consciousness, the traditional word for which is *spirit,* cannot be known in the normal sense of the word, and seeking it is futile. All knowing is within the realm of duality—subject and object, the knower and the known. The subject, the I, the knower without which nothing could be known, perceived, thought, or felt, must remain forever unknowable. This is because the 'I' has no form. Only forms can be known, and yet without the formless dimension, the world of form could not be. It is the luminous space in which the world arises and subsides. That space is the life that I Am. It is timeless. I Am timeless, eternal. What happens in that space is relative and temporary; pleasure and pain, gain and loss, birth and death.

If the meaning of living consciously is to remain aware, then self-acceptance is its major test. Self-acceptance is to be consciously aware of our experiences *in context* keeping an attitude that makes the concept of approval or disapproval irrelevant.

Self-acceptance is a precondition for change. If we accept the fact of what we feel, what we are, and who we are at any given moment, we can permit ourselves to be fully aware of the nature of our choices and actions. Thus, our personal development is not impeded. Remain aware!

Affirmation 14
I am freeing myself of all the negative mental programming by acknowledging the existence of secrets buried in my subconscious mind—secrets that have kept me from true happiness.

I am freeing myself of self-doubt, guilt, anxiety, fear, and unhappiness by exposing these secrets to those most affected, and to myself.

I am asking for forgiveness where I have harmed others and myself, and I choose to forgive those who have harmed me.

I am pleasing God, knowing He has already forgiven me for my transgressions and is providing the knowledge and guidance necessary to succeed within His plan for my life.

I am free of mental burdens that have for so long kept me from His will. I am one in the Spirit of Universe and I accept His reality in me.

20
The Formless Dimension

By looking deeper into reality, that is to say, to be exposed to scientific fact, you will discover the existence of the spirit dimension within yourself.

—Joel D. Johnson

CHANGING THE MENTAL picture that you hold of yourself and enhancing self-acceptance requires awareness of "what is." It requires compressing the myths held in captivity within the subconscious. It requires confronting those long held mentally programmed beliefs about yourself and others. It is time to face "what is" as what *really* is.

By looking deeper into reality, that is to say, to be exposed to scientific fact, you will discover the existence of the spirit dimension within yourself.

For instance, earlier we discussed the fact that there is no such thing as sound, color, texture, taste, or smell, as we have been programmed to believe they exist. This is counter to what most people believe; yet absence of sound, color, texture, smell, and taste outside the brain is a scientific and phenomenal fact. The fact is that everything we sense and perceive to be true about our life experiences only exists inside our own brain.

• • •

SENSORY REALITY
Most people believe that what they perceive as external sound is just that, external sound—that there is an actual noise produced, but is that so?

Random House Webster's College dictionary describes the word "sound" as *the <u>sensation</u> produced by stimulation of the organs of hearing by vibrations transmitted through the air or other medium*. In other words, when we speak we create silent vibrations with our vocal chords. In doing so we create unique vibrations that ebb and flow at various frequencies. These vibrating frequencies are picked up by the eardrums, which contain microscopic hairs that serve as sensory receptors. The brain translates the vibrations that the brain has been programmed to understand.

Dr. Rodolfo Llinas, Neuroscientist at The New York University Medical School, explains the reality of our senses:

> What the mind does, whether asleep or awake, is make images. But, these are purely mental constructions, even when they're based on external information. For example, light is nothing but electromagnetic radiation. Colors clearly don't exist outside our brains, nor does sound. Is there a sound if a tree drops in the forest and no one hears it? No! Sound is the relationship between external vibrations and the brain. If there is no brain, there can be no sound.
>
> This is true as it applies to touch, taste, and smell as well. The purpose of the sensory organs is to stimulate the brain in order for the mind to perceive events outside its self. If the brain is damaged, you may not experience certain

sensory stimulation such as sight, sounds, scents, taste, etc. If there is no brain, there can be no sight, sound, smell, texture or taste.

The upshot, says Llinas: "We can say that being awake or being conscious is nothing but a dreamlike state. It is a state that corresponds tightly to external reality. But, it has no objectable reality; as with a rainbow, you can perceive it, but never actually touch or measure it.

Perceptions and interpretations of life's events, both sensed and imagined, are stored in our subconscious. Memories are being made for future recall. This information is stored there to help us maneuver through life's pathways.

Coming to grips with "what is" means facing the truth about "what has been" as well. Moving sensed negative perceptions and enhanced interpretations from those compressed and suppressed mental files to the mental trashcan is necessary so that once and for all you do not have to deal with them.

Life does not always deal you what you might perceive as a good hand to play. Sometimes bad things happen, and although it is hard to understand, God does not put anything in your life that is not intended to move you toward your preordained purpose.

• • •

COMING TO GRIPS

Finally realizing and confronting the truth that lay deep within her subconscious mind, Mary reached out and came to grips with her past.

Between the ages of eight and ten-years-old, on more than one occasion her grandfather had sexually molested her. The molestation occurred on several occasions and she grew up with deep feelings of guilt and anger.

Mary is now married and the mother of four children. She was living out her daily life putting on an act of contentment and complete happiness, while living with her disturbing secret.

Ever since those horrible events occurred she felt used, dirty, consumed with guilt, and not fit as a human being. She often blamed herself and felt that somehow she was guilty of causing the molestations. She felt inadequate and lived her life in a world of semi make-believe and in denial.

Deep inside she felt as though she was an imposter. She believed her secret would soon be discovered and that she would have to deal with the dreaded confrontations. Mary believed she would be totally embarrassed. Her family would wonder why she had not already confessed this event. Why didn't she say something to someone when it happened? She had learned how to fool everyone, including herself.

As a little girl and many times as she grew to adulthood she wanted to tell someone, but she was afraid of what her father and mother and her husband might do when they found out that her grandfather had done these horrible things to her and perhaps to others as well.

She waited until her grandfather was on his deathbed before she finally told her husband. He convinced her she should open up to her mother and father and tell them exactly what happened. Mary finally gathered the nerve to face her demon and told her parents the gruesome details.

Of course, one can imagine the anger, hurt and shame her parent's felt. For several days everyone vented their feelings, which only added to her feelings of guilt for not coming forward sooner. The whole thing made her feel even nastier and more ashamed. The questions brought the obvious answer, "I was afraid of what people might think and what they might do."

Finally, Mary's father realized that no amount of anger, hatred for his father's actions, threats or physical confrontation, or anything else could change what had happened to his daughter. His dad was dying and it was too late for confrontation or legal action. It is a past event and nothing could be done that would change the molestation of his daughter. He could only forgive his dad and pray that God would forgive him, and that somehow his daughter would finally realize that what happened was not her fault.

Mary's father suggested that Mary and her husband go visit her grandfather, who at the age of seventy-eight was dying in a nursing home. Though he was unconscious, heavily medicated and unable to respond, Mary and her husband went to the nursing home and did as her dad suggested. Mary finally faced her guilt and partially compressed the event in her subconscious mind. She had finally confronted the guilt and anger she had carried with her all those years.

Mary told her grandfather that she has forgiven him for the horrible things he did to her and that she would pray for his soul. She realized, of course, that true forgiveness on her part and her parent's part would take time and that his ultimate punishment had to be in God's hands.

The memory of those childhood events and the disappointment and hatred she felt toward her grandfather had left her with fear and a feeling that all men are basically bad and are not to be trusted. She even wondered if her own father ever had sexual fantasies about her.

Mary was relieved to have exposed the truth concerning those events in her life and has now placed those events behind her. As life's events trigger those thoughts, she continues to compress those negative feelings that occasionally pop into her mind. After accepting what is as what is, she is finally working toward full self-acceptance and a strong self-image.

Now is the time to come to grips with your own magnified, negative interpretations of past events. It is time to face the truth and free yourself by affirming the positive new you.

Affirmation 15

I am living in God's favor. Past experiences have made me strong. I will face this moment and every moment hereafter with the knowledge that God loves me and has made me special for His purpose.

I am unique among all creatures in the entire universe. There is none other exactly like me and there will never be another exactly like me.

Though I am not complete, I am at this moment in time and space the person I am meant to be.

I am finding love, wisdom, and abundance through the Holy Spirit of the Universe that dwells in me. In His love I am being molded daily as a potter molds a uniquely beautiful vase. Everyone loves me. God loves me. God is with me always. In His love I AM.

I cannot fail.

21
Eliminating Bad Habits

Habits are an acquired pattern of behavior that can only be changed by replacing them with newly acquired patterns of behavior.

—**Joel D. Johnson**

ELIMINATING BAD HABITS is not easy. At least that has been my experience. No one ever told me it would be.

As an example, I think we could agree that smoking cigarettes is a disgusting habit that was once considered cool. For over thirty years I smoked almost two packs of cigarettes every day. No matter how hard I tried to kick the habit, it would not let go of me.

Renowned psychiatrist Sigmund Freud contends that oral fixations such as thumb sucking, gum chewing, chewing tobacco and smoking are the results of an uncompleted oral stage. Based on Freud, I may have been weaned too soon, which caused a constant desire to put something in my mouth. I am ashamed to admit it, but I also bit my nails. It is confession time here.

There seemingly is never enough to quench the psychosexual desire that Freud talks about. None-the- less, I had to quit!

I had a horribly hacking cough. My breath stunk, my clothes stunk, I stunk, and my love life stunk. I really had to quit. I had to choose between cigarettes and my family, between being controlled by an object that had no mind of its own and those that did. I had to be free of cigarettes and the guilt that smoking carried with it. Quitting was a thing I *had to have.*

Thank God, my marriage survived. I finally realized that my 'rock bottom,' as far as our marriage was concerned, was closer than I had wanted to admit.

Headaches were constant. At times they were so bad I would get sick to my stomach. I had convinced myself that the headaches were migraines I must have inherited from my father. My dad had been a smoker and suffered all his life with severe headaches, but we would not believe smoking cigarettes was the cause.

It's in the trees, the grass, the cat, the weather or something. I'm probably allergic to the pine tree's, that's all. It could not possibly be cigarettes. Good grief, they have filters on those things. "Back off! I'll be fine," I thought.

I did not understand.

The fear of death is not what made me quit. It was the realization that by smoking cigarettes I was pushing my family away, the people I loved more than life itself. I was forcing them to breathe the cigarette smoke that I exhaled. It is a horrible habit. There is no telling how many clients I lost due to smoking cigarettes.

Finally realizing something had to be done, I decided to pray about it and look for some guidance through reading the word of God, the Holy Bible.

My mother told me once that if I was looking for answers to one of life's challenges that all I need do is close my eyes, open the Bible, and place my finger on the page that was open. Then all I had to do was open my eyes and read the words where my finger had landed. So I thought I would try this magical thing. I opened my eyes and read the words from the King James Version of the Bible. My finger had landed on the 'Parable of the Sower', Luke 8:5-16. Of course, Jesus was talking about salvation, but I am sure he meant we would also reap whatever we sow. The results required belief, translation, and understanding, but brought me some comfort. We have to listen to our moms.

One day on the way to visit a client, I reached in my shirt pocket for one of those nasty things. As I pulled the recently purchased pack of cigarettes from my pocket, I glanced down at my steering wheel where I had taped one of my business cards. On the back of the business card I had printed in bold type, I AM NOT A SMOKER. Anyone can do anything one day at a time, I told myself. As I held the pack in the palm of my left hand, it suddenly dawned on me that cigarettes were controlling me. I can think! They can't! I was getting angry with myself.

I said to myself, "Not knowing is ignorance. Knowing and doing it anyway is called stupid. What does that make me?" I was not aware that I had an oral fixation as a result of an uncompleted oral stage. I was not aware that I had a desire to breastfeed.

I knew the rules: The first step in eliminating bad habits is to admit that you have a bad habit. You must first come to grips with that fact. Until you realize you are addicted and freely admit it to yourself, it will be extremely difficult to quit. I was obsessed with the desire to smoke. I was a cigarette addict. Not good!

I took one more look at the cigarettes, rolled the car window down and threw the pack out the window as I yelled at the top of my voice, "I CONTROL ME! FROM THIS DAY FORWARD YOU WILL NEVER CONTROL ME AGAIN."

At the time, it was the same as throwing seventy-five cents out of the window. Under normal circumstances I would never have thrown seventy-five cents out any window. I would not have thrown a penny out of the window.

I was really proud of myself. I reread the card. I AM NOT A SMOKER. I read it several times. As I drove down the highway, every time I had withdrawals I read the affirmation.

About an hour later I was reading it for about the fifteenth time as I pulled up to the convenience store. The pain in my stomach was horrible. I was having withdrawal pains on top of withdrawal pains. "I'm a dope addict," I thought. "What's going to happen to me?" (negative affirmations) Some folks never experience withdrawal pains. They just quit and that's that. Nothing to it! I was really hooked.

"A pack of cigarettes please," I asked the cashier. As she reached for the cigarettes, I had the urge to tell her to forget it and that I was quitting. But, I didn't. I paid her and tore the pack open as I rushed back to the van to light up. I can't describe the relief I felt as I inhaled the first puff. I felt guilty. "I am a sinner and a liar." (more negative affirmations) "If this is how an addict feels, it has to be a horrible way to live," I thought.

As I pulled out of the convenience store parking lot onto the highway, I glanced at the card again. I AM NOT A SMOKER.

When the pain had subsided, and as I coughed the fourth or fifth time, I said to the pack of cigarettes, "OK, so you're trying to show me who the boss is. Well, I'm going show *YOU* who the boss is. *I'm the boss*. That's who the boss is. I'm going to win this battle. I'll smoke just three of you a day for one week, and every time I light up I'll read my card. I AM NOT A SMOKER. The next week I'll smoke two cigarettes each day and read the card. The next week I'll smoke one each day and read the card. From then on, I'll be free."

Again, I was so proud of myself. I had a plan. The pain was gone, but not the cough. I had convinced myself I would win this battle. It should be so easy. I thought of how proud my family was going to be. My wife was going to love me to death for licking this horrible habit, which was reason strong enough to quit. "She will be very proud," I thought.

As I was driving down the highway and thinking about this, I glanced at the card once more. I had only taken a few puffs as I looked at my affirmation, I AM NOT A SMOKER, then threw the cigarette out the window. Normally, I smoked a cigarette almost all the way to the filter, which I later discovered was caused by mental programming I had received as a child. Every time we sat down as a family to eat a meal together, mom would say, "Eat everything on your plate. Don't be wasteful. Just remember there are starving kids all over the world digging in trashcans to get a little taste of what you are eating and you have plenty. You should be ashamed. Eat it all! We are not going to throw good food away."

I once got my ears boxed for saying, "Well, we could wrap this stuff up in foil, put it in a box, and send it overseas so they could have some too." Thus, I chose to not waste any cigarette puffs.

I turned on the radio in an effort to get my mind off the cigarettes. It was now two o'clock in the afternoon, and my next cigarette would be right before bedtime, about 10 P.M. "Surely, I could wait until then. I will suffer a little, but I can make it till 10 P.M," I thought to myself, as I listened to the calming easy listening music.

Another hour had passed, and I began to feel those horrible withdrawal pains again. I started to give in and reached for the pack. "No, I will not give in!"

My stomach tightened at the very thought of having to wait. I bent over the steering wheel, gritting my teeth. The more I thought about it, the more I realized how weak I was. Waiting any longer was out of the question. I had to have another cigarette. I thought of that country song by Tex Williams, *"Smoke, Smoke, Smoke, That Cigarette.* "What a weak person I am," I thought as I lit up the cigarette. (another negative affirmation) Feeling guilt, I glanced at the words on my card, I AM NOT A SMOKER.

Knowing in my heart I had to quit smoking and realizing nothing was going to happen until I made a final decision to do so, I took two long puffs and threw the cigarette out the window. Then I reached for the new pack and threw it out the window, along with my lighter. I glanced at the card once more...I AM NOT A SMOKER.

"NOW" I said to myself, "I don't care how much pain I have, cigarettes are not going to control me. NO PAIN...NO GAIN."

Trying to get my mind off the desire to smoke, I stared down the long stretch of highway between Abilene and Lubbock. I could see what seemed to be thousands of acres of new cotton on both sides of the highway. Occasionally, I saw irrigation sprinklers watering the parched land.

It was flat land, dusty and ugly, and yet it was beautiful too. Maybe that's why people stayed. It had an unusually nostalgic beauty about it. It reminded me of the Dust Bowl of the late 1930s and the Great Depression. It reminded me of the multitude of migrant farm workers looking for work to keep their families fed. How difficult that must have been for them back then. I could almost see the ragged old wagons, pickups, and cars with personal belongings in the trunk and packed high on the roof, headed for what they believed would be a better life.

Hundreds of workers ended up in migrant worker camps where fifty-cents a day would have been considered good pay. I thought how I had just thrown more than that out the window. I wasn't worried about what my children were going to eat or where we would sleep that night, but I had a feeling of guilt creep into my mind as I thought about the challenges those good folks had. The movie *Grapes of Wrath* came to mind.

At the tail end of the depression and right before WW II, when I was a small child my family was part of that scene. My mom and dad ventured as far as Lamesa, Texas, in their effort to find a better life, but it was not to be. They stayed with kinfolk for a while, but soon discovered life was not greener on the other side of the fence. So they turned around and came back to East Texas where life was not nearly as bad as the so-called "promised land".

As I continued my trip between Abilene and Lubbock, I noticed a group of what I perceived to be buildings or grain storage facilities way off in the distance. I was not sure of what it was, but it amazed me that I could see that far. The flatness seemed to go forever. There were hardly any trees at all.

"A man could get hypnotized driving on this straight highway and watching that white line," I thought, as I was doing everything I could to keep my mind off cigarettes.

I looked at the card again...I AM NOT A SMOKER.

I continued to stare at the shapes way off in the distance as they got bigger and bigger, curious to know what they would finally end up being. Concentrating on the shapes was making me sleepy. "Coffee, that's what I need...coffee."

"Cup of coffee," I said to the waitress in the old country café.

"How is business around here?" I asked, trying to strike up a conversation. "It gets mighty lonely on the road."

As she sat the coffee in front of me the waitress smiled and said, "Some days are good, some days are bad. Depends on the weather. Right now it is very hot, as you know. Business has been pretty good. Everybody wants to come in out of the heat."

"I don't live around this part of the state. I am from East Texas. We have lots of trees. How do you stand it? I mean no trees, high winds, dust, heat and more dust, and the tumbleweeds are so big they could wreck you car. I've been dodging them for miles. It's flat as a flitter as far as I can see in any direction."

"Oh, I suppose you just get used to it," she said.

"Well, tell me one thing that you like about this part of Texas," I asked, grinning.

"I ain't thought about it much, but I suppose there is one thing about it. Kids can run away from home, and you can watch'em for three days."

We had a good laugh. I wondered how many times she had told that one.

I reached in my pocket for a cigarette and realized I had thrown them out the window, along with my lighter. A cigarette vending machine stood against the wall. The pain began as the thought of cigarettes captured my mind. It was as though someone had grabbed hold of me and was stabbing me with an ice pick. I wanted to lay on the floor in a fetal position, but I finished my coffee, said goodbye, and got back in the van. I left the café as fast as I could, leaving a large dust cloud behind me as I pulled off the gravel lot.

I drove down the highway a few miles fighting stomach cramps. The withdrawals were really getting to me. Thinking a short walk might help, I pulled off the highway. After getting out of the van, I walked a few steps and then I trotted a few steps, turned and trotted back toward the van. It seemed to help a little bit.

A truckload of farm workers drove by. One of the workers thumped a lit cigarette onto the highway. "Oh, my gosh! Someone up there must be listening," I thought. I waved as I continued trotting back and forth. The workers must have thought I was crazy. I watched until they got out of sight.

After I knew they couldn't see me, I looked both ways to see if any cars were coming. There were none. I ran to the cigarette, picked it up and took a long hard draw. Then realizing that I might have just contacted someone's horrible disease, I threw it down.

I ran back to the van. A sharp pain struck my stomach as I glanced at the card once more. I AM NOT A SMOKER.

Yeah...right! I pulled back onto the highway and ripped the card off the horn, ripped it up and tossed it in my trash box. My brain was yelling at me, "Where is my nicotine?"

Realizing my mistake of throwing out my affirmation, I prayed that God would give me the strength to quit. Once more I pulled off the highway and removed a business card from my pocket. I placed it on the steering wheel. In large letters I printed on the back I AM NOT A SMOKER. After placing the card on the clip that held my sunglasses to the sun visor, I paused and read it several times.

It had been a while since I had my last cigarette. I didn't know how much longer I could hold out. "Louise would never understand this. It's best I don't even mention it," I thought.

Finally, I was approaching a small town. I pulled up to a local convenience store, got out of the car and placed the fuel nozzle in my gas tank and rushed into the store.

"Give me..." I hesitated! "Listen, I'm trying to quit smoking, but I'm having withdrawals pains like a dope addict."

The attendant laughed, "I know what you mean. I've been there... done that. I had 'em bad. I used smokeless tobacco to help me get past it."

"What's that?" I asked. I thought this must be something new. I had never heard of smokeless tobacco.

"Man...that would be great if it would work. What is it?" I asked.

"It is tobacco in a pouch. It's fairly new. Been around for a few months," he said.

"How does that work?"

"Well, you put a pouch between your gums...sort of like chewing tobacco, only it's not chewing tobacco. It's like cigarette tobacco in a little pouch. Here, I'll show you," he said, while handing me a round can that contained several small white pouches filled with tobacco.

"Man that could cause cancer of the mouth. I don't want to do that and besides, I hate dipping and chewing."

"Okay! What else can I do for you?" His facial expression told me he didn't believe I was serious about quitting.

For the longest, I just stood there thinking, should I or shouldn't I? "That stuff is going to taste terrible with coffee," I said, smiling. "I can't let anything stand between me and my coffee. That's for sure, but I can't smoke cigarettes anymore. I've got to beat this thing. Are you sure that will work?"

"I'm not promising anything. I can only tell you it worked for me."

"Alright, I'll try,"

"Better get you a spit cup with some paper in it. You don't want to spit out the window while you are going down the highway, it could mess up your clothes and your car and you sure don't want to swallow this stuff," he laughed.

"When you feel the cramps coming on, put one between you gums. Just leave it there for as long as you can, even after all the juice is gone, and pretty soon you won't need'em any more, the pouches or cigarettes."

After several days the cramps began to subside. I had gone four days without a cigarette.

I read my affirmations four times each day and aloud just before I retired for the night and other times as well. The affirmation was on my mind constantly, especially each time I opened the can to take out a pouch of smokeless tobacco.

After a few weeks I noticed I was keeping the pouch in my mouth way past the disposal period and had no withdrawals at all. I was unconsciously weaning myself.

After going through that experience, I learned a valuable lesson about habits. To eliminate a habit, you have to replace it with another habit.

I HAD WON. Was it because I was forced to quit? Was it because the smokeless pouch eliminated the desire to reach into my pocket for that pack of cigarettes? Had I fooled my mind and body into thinking I am not a smoker? While those reasons definitely played a major part, I believe, in the final analysis, it was the affirmation that did the trick. Affirmations without action can lead to depression and guilt. Will this work for you…only if you believe.

I AM NOT A SMOKER is a powerful affirmation. If you are a smoker, these five words are now imbedded in your subconscious. Each time you reach for the cigarettes in your pocket or light up, you will automatically repeat, I AM NOT A SMOKER.

You know you should not be smoking. You know it is not healthy. Your feelings of guilt will haunt you until you finally decide to quit.

If you are a drinker simply replace the word 'smoker' with the word 'drinker'. I AM NOT A DRINKER. You too can change…if you *have to have* it badly enough.

• • •

LOSING WEIGHT
According to Aetna InteliHealth in *Stopping that Rebound in Weight*:

> It's an unfortunate fact that most people who lose a significant amount of weight gain a significant amount of it back over time. Statistics show that up to 90% of people who lose weight regain it back within five years.

Why is weight maintenance so difficult? There's a theory that you have a genetically pre-determined set point, a weight at which your body tries to maintain. When you deviate too far from this set point, your body sabotages your weight loss attempt by boosting your appetite and decreasing your activity level. A recent study published in the New England Journal of Medicine confirms this idea.

Researchers in Australia recruited fifty obese and overweight people to participate in a calorie restricted diet and exercise program to lose weight. Over the course of the 10-week program, the participants lost an average of 14% of their body weight. Unfortunately, when they followed up with the "successful losers" sixty weeks later, they had regained almost half of the weight they had lost.

Unless you have reprogrammed your subconscious mind and have compressed the negative thoughts, no matter how many diets you try, you will most likely return to your pre-determined weight, with additional pounds you may not want. Diets can help you to lose weight for a short period of time, but they do not work over the long term unless the diet becomes habit. The wrong diet may also be bad for your health.

For a long time, I thought I would always be skinny. Most of my life I weighed 155 pounds dripping wet. That is, until I reached forty-years-old. Then one day, for what seemed to be without warning, I looked down and could not find my feet. I had developed the furniture disease. You know, when your chest falls into your drawers. Pregnant women had nothing on me. I could relate. I knew what it felt like to carry around that ten-pound baby.

My work habits had changed. I no longer lifted heavy cases or moved at a fast pace. I was now traveling five states, which required sitting and driving for long periods of time. I was not burning the fat like before. I thought, "Well, finally, I'm putting some weight on. Maybe there's nothing wrong with me after all."

After I quit smoking my taste buds changed! I actually like liver now, if you can believe that, and spinach, too. I couldn't believe it. I went from a size thirty-two pant to a size forty-four. My neck size grew from fourteen and a half to a seventeen. The weight gain finally stopped at 223 pounds, and I began to maintain that weight mostly around the midsection. So once again I created a new affirmation in order to reprogram my subconscious mind.

The subconscious begins its work the moment it accepts your affirmations as fact. It will not just suddenly happen. It will take time. Be patient!

An affirmation can help you develop new lifestyle choices that will keep the weight off and help you live a healthy, happier life.

When preparing your meals or eating out, you will begin to automatically choose foods that are good for you. If you don't make the right choices, guilt will haunt you every day until you change. No one said it would be easy.

We over eat, smoke, drink, etc. to satisfy hidden psychological desires. Those desires can only be satisfied when healthy choices are imbedded in the subconscious mind. Don't let emotion and fear stop you. Just say I AM.

Affirmation 16
I am eliminating bad habits that for too long have made me feel weak and have reduced my ability to enjoy a healthy life style.

I am creating positive I AM statements of faith and activating the power in those affirmations to eliminate unnecessary habits. I now realize that for my life to be whole, I must change.

I am releasing myself from the bondage of emotional guilt, fear, and anxiety, realizing the mental baggage that has held me back for so long no longer has power over me.

I am releasing myself from bondage to the past and fear of the future. I know that the past is only a memory right now and the future is only a thought that will never come because there is only now.

I am successful.

22
Eliminating Fear

You gain strength, courage, and confidence by every experience in which you must stop and look fear in the face. You must do the thing you think you cannot do.

—**Eleanor Roosevelt**

FEAR IS AN emotion induced by a perceived threat or by anticipation of anger or pain. The perceived threat causes the mammalian brain to inject adrenalin into the body causing the natural reflexes to pull away or flee. While there are often obvious reasons to fear an action from a thing or someone, in many instances fear is simply False Evidence Appearing Real.

We are born with only two fears: the fear of falling and the fear of loud noises. All other fears are learned through experience and self-talk.

Emotions are strong feelings concerning how we feel about a certain thing. Emotions are expressed as love, anger, joy, hate or fear. How we feel manipulates conscious thought and, thus, has the potential to control our actions.

THE POWER OF SELF-IMAGING

The subconscious mind is programmed best when strong emotions are attached to an action. We tend to be able to recall those things that are emotionally exaggerated for a very long period of time. Fear is no exception.

Advertising experts go to great length to study what makes people do what they do and buy what they buy. They study likes and dislikes and what makes people tick. They want to find out what one's hot buttons are—when and how to push them. Their studies show that people want to feel good about themselves. People want to feel as though they are liked, respected, accepted, popular, and successful. They want to look good to their friends and to the world.

Ego is constantly in a state of wanting more and more of everything. Ego can never get enough. Advertising experts want to know how you are controlled by your ego, and if so, what turns your ego on.

Experts have found that by subliminally exaggerating mental pictures of their products and their value, while pushing the emotional hot button of the potential customer, a desire to buy is created. That is why you continually see and hear the same seemingly foolish and exaggerated advertising over and over. Stimulating the desire to buy is not so much about the product as it is how customers believe the product will make them feel. Customers have been programmed.

Some of the things you fear right now were programmed into your subconscious when you were a small child. Remember being afraid of the dark or being afraid that something was under your bed, or that you would wake up one day and find your parents have moved and left you behind? Where do you think fears like those come from? They come from false perceptions and interpretations. They come from observation and self-talk.

Why, as an adult, do you continue to fear those things? Why is it necessary that you sleep with a light on or have to have the television on before you can fall asleep? Why do you look around your room or lock the door before you go to bed? You've been programmed!

The following is an example of exaggerated programming through advertising: What product uses frogs and Clydesdale horses in their advertising? Beer, of course! What company uses a lizard in their marketing campaign? You know the answer, don't you? Insurance!

Advertisers learned long ago that jingles help to cement a brand or product into a potential buyer's mind, while creating a desire to buy. Key words and phrases are often used to subliminally program us to take action. That is why we often reach for the product that is imbedded in our subconscious.

Remember these? "_____, taste good like a cigarette should." Can you guess the brand?

"Hmm, hmm, good…hmm, hmm, good…that's what _____ is…hmm, hmm, good." Can you fill in the blanks? These cigarette and soup commercials were popular in the sixties. After more than fifty years many of us still remember these commercials.

Just like in advertising, subliminally exaggerated fears can influence decisions for a lifetime. The fear of loss, the fear of rejection, the fear of failure, the fear of success, the fear of not being accepted, the fear of not being loved, the fear of dying, the fear of being trapped or enclosed, and the fear of flying, are some of the many programmed fears. If exaggerated strongly enough, these fears can become very difficult to overcome. In the end though, we must realize fear is simply False Evidence Appearing Real.

My wife and I have a friend I will refer to as Nancy. Nancy has a tremendous fear of flying in an airplane. This fear is called aerophobia. Over many years of reading about and watching television reports of airplane crashes, Nancy believes she will be one of the unlucky passengers who will go down with the plane.

After much discussion and much encouragement, coupled with our emotional plea, Louise and I finally convinced Nancy and her husband to fly to Nashville with us. One of our best jobs of selling, I must say. No doubt, even now, the dented armrests left by her tight grip are still a subject of discussion among the airline's executives. I hesitate to mention the name of the airline for fear they may be looking for her.

Nancy's imagination, along with her fear of flying, caused her to perspire the entire trip. Surely there was no dry spot on her body. She could hardly wait until we landed. She wanted to kiss the ground when she got off the plane. Fortunately, the trip back was much more relaxed and she seemed to be enjoying the flight, though to our knowledge she has not flown since. This incident exemplifies that emotion, how one feels about things, is a powerful selling tool.

An emotional appeal and its effect on one's intellect, combined with the fear of loss, can have an almost hypnotic effect on people. It was a trick Hitler used to mesmerize millions of German citizens prior to and during World War II. In fact, emotional appeals have been exercised in the political arena throughout history.

A person who aspires to become a good salesperson should take lessons from history and from advertising research. Enthusiastically appealing to a person's emotions with slightly exaggerated visuals and sounds is highly contagious. Selling is simply the process of transferring one's enthusiasm for a product, an idea, or service to a potential buyer. Hitler understood very well.

We tend to remember events that are tied to powerful emotion. I've never forgotten the day my dad threw me in the creek. It was a very traumatic and emotional event in my life. For years I was afraid of both water and my Dad. I had nightmares of him holding my head under water and drowning me.

My dad never burned me with cigarettes, tied me to the bed, locked me in a closet, or deprived me of food for days or hours on end. And most of the time the lickings I got, I deserved. He could have hurt me physically, but he didn't. But, I can describe in detail the belt he used down to the color, size, buckle and holes it contained. Also, I can give detailed accounts of the events that caused me to get a whipping.

I was not victimized, although I felt like a victim at times as a result of my own self-talk. Nonetheless, where strong emotion was attached to the discipline I received, I never forgot it. You most likely have not forgotten your punishments either.

I can't blame my dad, my teachers, my siblings or anyone else. They, too, were programmed and had their own challenges to deal with. By acknowledging the thoughts were mine and by reading my affirmations, I was able to compress those deeply embedded feelings. I have now moved on with my life.

You may think little emotional events that cause you to fear trying have had no effect on you, thus you are not concerned with them. You are possibly saying, "That was the past. Now is now, and that part of my life is over." These emotional events, however, remain in your subconscious and in your daily thoughts. Unless you have dug up and *compressed* the events that you hold secret within, like weeds in your garden, they will come up and damage your crop. You may even catch the *I can't disease*. Don't let that happen to you. Weed your garden!

23
The Final Analysis

Look well into yourself; there is a source, which will always spring up if you will search there.

—Marcus Antoninus

IT IS MY desire that *The Power of Self-Imaging* will help you come to realize that you are more than what you may currently perceive as your reality. It should also help you recognize and change false interpretations of events that may have haunted you for a lifetime.

You are a spirit being within a physical form. You experience what you perceive to be your own reality only one nanosecond at a time in the consciousness of our mind. You are part of the universal fabric of all that is, not separate or alone, but a part of what is and ever will be.

Michael Brown, spiritual leader and author of *The Presence Process*, says:

> There is a gap between every other human being and us. This gap is the space between us. This gap appears real

because of our physical body. In the gap between everyone else and us is where the world manifests. What we call 'our world' is this gap.

Because our physical body leads us to believe that this gap is real, we automatically believe that we can be separated from others. We believe that our body is separate from the bodies of others and that we therefore have our own physical sensations. We believe that we have our own mind and therefore our own thoughts. We believe that we have our own heart and therefore our own emotions. We believe that we have our own spirit and therefore our own spiritual experiences. This perception leads us to believe that when we are not in the company of another human being, we are therefore on our own. Having a physical body allows us to believe that we can be alone.

The proof inherent in these Oneness experiences reveals to us:

- That our physical bodies, though appearing separate, are not; they are connected energetically somehow to every other body.
- That our mind is not the physical brain in our head; its capacities extend beyond the confines of our physical bodies to any distance that we care to think about.
- That our emotional experiences are not confined to us alone; they are shared by the world around us.
- That our ongoing and unfolding spiritual awareness is not personal or exclusive; it is universal and inclusive.

So it is then that we should recognize the fact that each human being, though appearing separate, is one with all there is. Each of is a living Spirit Being united with the Spirit of the Universe…God.

You must understand that those events that are stored in your subconscious that have convinced you that you are no *good* or that you *will never amount to a hill of beans* are not true. You must realize you are already the very essence of God and you have the power within you to achieve anything you choose.

Albert Einstein says:

> A human being is a part of the whole, called by us the 'universe', a part limited in time and space. He experiences himself, his thoughts and feelings, as something separate from the rest—a kind of optical delusion of his consciousness. This delusion is a kind of prison for us, restricting us to our personal desires and to affection for a few persons nearest to us. Our task must be to free ourselves from this prison by widening our circle of compassion to embrace all living creatures and the whole of nature in its beauty. Nobody is able to achieve this completely, but the striving for such achievement is in itself a part of the liberation and a foundation for inner security.

You have your own unique stories that you have embellished. These stories over time that you have added to and subtracted from are so mixed with all other events now stored in your subconscious mind that you may be confused about what is real and what is not. Realize that you must free yourself from the false evidence now appearing real within your subconscious mind and release the false stories, the secrets in your closet, to the world. Until you do, it will be extremely difficult to develop a self-image that truly represents the essence of who and what you are.

Don't hold your mind prisoner to the past or hold fearful dreams of the future. Know that you are a very special creation with the power of the universe within you. Understand it, grasp it, and live in it one moment-at-a-time.

In the Holy Bible, Mark 22-25: Jesus said to the disciples:

> I tell you the truth, you can say to this mountain, 'May you be lifted up and thrown into the sea,' and it will happen. But

you must really believe it will happen and have no doubt in your heart. I tell you, you can pray for anything, and *if you believe that you've received it, it will be yours.* But when you are praying, first forgive anyone you are beholding a grudge against, so that your Father in heaven will forgive your sins, too.

Have faith! You have the power of self-imaging within.

About the Author

JOEL D. JOHNSON

Since high school Joel has had an inexhaustible hunger to know who we are, what we are, and why we are here; physically, spiritually and scientifically. He has spent a great portion of his life in his spare time studying this subject.

Joel's first book was *The American Dream is Success in a Business of Your Own*, a guide for starting a business, which was published in 1994 by G Randall Publishing Co.

He has written several articles concerning business advice, public interest, and personal development that have appeared in various newspapers and magazines including, *Footwear News*, a division of Fairchild Publishing Co., *The Longview News-Journal*, and *The East Texas Review*. You can read more recent articles in his personal blog at *www.joelconsult.blog.com*.

Following graduation from Tyler High School, he was made manager of a shoe store in Dallas, TX, and later he operated stores in Shreveport, LA, Ft. Worth, TX, Columbus, GA, and Houston, TX. In May of 1963 he decided to go into business for himself and established J & J Shoes, Inc. and grew the business to include twelve locations in three states (TX, AR, LA).

In 1976 he became a independent footwear representative and traveled five states (TX, LA, AR, OK, NM) representing two lines of women's footwear. During that time he attended continuing education classes and became a Certified Footwear Representative with the designation of CFR.

In 1996 he retired from the footwear industry. Retirement was not suitable to his nature and later that year he was hired by Kilgore College Small Business Development Center as a business counselor in Longview, TX. While associated with KCSBDC he earned certification as Senior Business Development Specialist. He also occasionally taught continuing education classes at Kilgore College's Longview Center, in the subjects of marketing and salesmanship.

Shortly after leaving KCSBDC in 2001, he established Joel Johnson and Associates, a management and marketing consulting company. His mission is to provide business and personal solutions for survival and beyond. He continues to focus on serving individuals and business clients on a confidential basis.

Joel has been happily married to Louise Ladatta Johnson for more than sixty years. They have four children, two boys and two girls and nine grandchildren. Joel and Louise live in East Texas, in the beautiful city of Longview, Texas.

Resources

Benjamin Disraeli
Joel Johnson, author, *The Power of Self-Imaging*, P. 5
Frank S. Murphy, D.O., Psychiatrist, Author of *Power Without Pills* – Review.
Deepok Chopra, M. D. Author - *Ageless Body, Timeless Mind*, Harmony Books, 1993, ISBN 0-517-59257-6, P. 10
Proverbs 20:24, *The Holy Bible, King James Version*, Thomas Nelson Publisher, 1976, Giant Print, ISBN 7- 789-10888-9-0, P. 990,
Albert Einstein
Eckhart Tolle, author, *A New Earth*, (The Illusory self), Plum Books, ISBN 978-0-452-28996-3, P.27 -28
Ken Wilber, author, *Integral Psychology*-1998- ISBN 10-1-5062-554- 9, P.33
Luke 11:9, *The Holy Bible, King James Version*, Thomas Nelson Publisher, 1976, Giant Print, ISBN 7-789-10888-9-0, P. 1514
Ralph Waldo Emerson, also attributed to **Albert Jay Nock**, author of *Meditations in Wall Street*, 1940, Publisher William Morrow & Company
Maxwell Maltz, M. D., F.I.C.S., author, **Psycho-cybernetics**, 1960- Prentice-Hall, Inc., ISBN 0-671-22150-7, P. 31
2 Corinthians-5: 1-5, *Life Application Study Bible, New Living Translation*, Second Addition, Tyndale House Publishers, Inc. ISBN 1-4143-0213-4, P. 1966

Luke 17:20-21, *The Holy Bible, King James Version,* Thomas Nelson Publisher, 1976, Giant Print, ISBN 7-789-10888-9-0 P. 1527-

Islam: www.n1uslim.org The Hahore Ahmadiyya Movement (48)

Aish Rabbi - Judaism: - From *The Teachings of Judaism* - www.aish.com. "The Afterlife"

Buddhism: Yen Thich Nguyen Tang, *Buddhist View on Death and Rebirth,* 1/I1. www.urbandl}ara:omudha;rma***tewdeath.html

Eve Wilson, Spiritual teacher, *Wherever You Are* - www.spiritualhealers.com

Sarah Dessen, Author of *What Happened to Goodbye,* 2011, Published by Penquin Group, ISBN 978-110-15286-4-8

Michel De Montaigne, French writer and philosopher, 1533-1592, Tilde A. Sankovitch, Biographer, Britannica.

Earl Nightingale- Earl Nightingale Quotes

Eckhart Tolle, Author of *The Power of Now,* Namaste Publishing, 1997 and the New World Library, 1999, ISBN 1- **57731**-480-8, P.17

Proverbs 23:7, *The Holy Bible, King James Version,* Thomas Nelson Publisher, 1976, Giant Print, ISBN 7-789-10888-9-0 P.992

Joseph Murphy, Ph.D, D.O., *The Power of the Subconscious* (Revised by Ian McMahan Ph.D. Reward Books, Paramus, N.J. _ ISBN 0-7352-0168-4 - P. 10

Julie K. Hersh, author of *Struck by Living, From Depression to Hope,* Brown Books Publishing Group, ISBN 13-978-1- 934812-63-1 & ISBN 10: 1-934812-63-3, (Inside sleeve, front cover)

Joshua Loth Leibman, Quotes

Joel D. Johnson

Richard M. DeVos, President Amway Corp.

St. Augustine

W. Somerset Maugham

Deepok Chopra, M. D., author of, *Ageless Body, Timeless Mind,* Harmony Books, 1993, ISBN 0-517-59257-6, P. 25.

Matthew 17:20, *The Holy Bible, King James Version,* Thomas Nelson Publisher,

Joel Johnson, author of *The Power of Self-Imaging*.
Eckhart Tolle, author of *A New Earth*, Published by the Penguin Group, A Plume Book, ISBN 978-0-452-28996-3.
William James, 18th century psychologist
Dale Carnegie, author of *How to Win Friends and Influence People*, Copyright 1936, published 1952, Simon & Schuster, original 71st Printing, ISBN 0-671-02703-4, P. l02.
Robert Collier
Abraham Lincoln
Dale Carnegie, author of *How to Win Friends and Influence People*, Copyright 1936, published 1952, Simon & Schuster, original 71st Printing, ISBN 0-671-02703-4, P. l03.
1 Corinthians-2: 9-12 - *Life Application Study Bible*, New Living Translation, Second Addition, Tyndale House Publishers, Inc. ISBN 1-4143-0213-4, P.1930
Jeremy Bentham
Bill Britt, successful entrepreneur
F. W. Boreham
Jim Rohn
Susan A. Greenfield, author of *The Human Brain* ISBN 0-465-00736-0
Leslie H. Hart, author of, *How the Brain Works*, ISBN 13-978- 1929869008,
Maxwell Maltz, M.D., author of, *Psycho-Cybernetics*, ISBN 0-671-22150-7, P.12
John Medina, author *of Brain Rules*- ISBN 978-9-9707777-0-7
Sir John C. Eccles, British neurologist,
Wikipedia.org - Typoglycemia
David B. Chamberlain, editor of, Prenatal Memory and Learning. author of *Windows to the Womb*, North Atlantic Books, Berkeley, CA -ISBN 978-1-58394-551-3
Webster's Universal College Dictionary
Charles Haanel, author of, *The Master Key System*, 2007, BN Publishing, ISBN 9562910881
Nikola Tesla, Inventory, From: Charles Haanel, author of, *The Master Key System*, 2007, BN Publishing, ISBN 9562910881-Part seven, Item 10. P. 41

Socrates, 469-399 B.C.
Jim Rohn, motivation speaker, author, and mentor to the masters, audio *The Challenge to Succeed.*
Anthony Robbins, author of, Awaken The Giant Within- Simon & Schuster, 1991, ISBN 0-671-72734-6, P. 25
Earl Nightingale
Proverbs 6:2 - *The Holy Bible, King James Version*, Thomas Nelson Publisher,
Albert Einstein
Leslie H. Hart, author of, *How The Brain Works*, 1975, the University of Michigan, ISBN 0465031021, P.l08
Leslie H. Hart, author of, *How The Brain Works*, 1975, the University of Michigan, ISBN 0465031021
Rit Nosotro, author of *History of Textbook Propaganda*
Thomas Cooley
Dr. John Dewy, one of America's most profound philosophers
Galatians 6:7 - *The Holy Bible, King James Version*, Thomas Nelson Publisher,
J.D. Adams, *The Nature of Premises/Creating Ideal Personal Futures*
Joel Johnson, author of *The Power of Self-Imaging*
Albert Einstein
Maxwell Maltz, M.D., author of, *Psycho-Cybernetics*, 1960, Printice-Hall, Inc., a Fireside Book, ISBN 0-671-22150-7
Maxwell Maltz, M.D., author of, *Psycho-Cybernetics*, 1960, Printice-Hall, Inc., a Fireside Book, ISBN 0-671-22150-7
Michael Brown, author of, *The Presence Process*, 2005, Namaste Publishing/ Beaufort Books, ISBN 0-8253-0537-3 P. 124
Eckhart Tolle, author of, *The Power of Now* – ISBN -978-1-57731-480-6 P.116
Eckhart Tolle, author of, *A New Earth, Awakening to Your life's Purpose*, 2005, Plume Books, Ltd, a Penquin Group, ISBN 9780-452- 28996-3, P. 242
Nathaniel Branden, PhD
Random House Webster's College Dictionary 1991-92, ISBN 0-679-41420-7, P. 1278
Dr. Rodulfo Llinas, Neuroscientist

Joel Johnson, author of *The Power of Self-Imaging*
Sigmund Freud
Tex Williams
Aetna InteliHealth, *Stopping that Rebound in Weight*, New England Journal of Medicine, 2012
Eleanor Roosevelt
Marcus Antoninus
Michael Brown, spiritual leader and author of *The Presence Process*, 2005, Namaste Publishing, ISBN 10-0-8253-0537-3 P.253
Albert Einstein
Mark 11: 22-25, Holy Bible, *Life Application Study Bible, New Living Translation*, Second Addition, Tyndale House Publishers, Inc. ISBN 1-4143-0213-4, P. 1646

For more information concerning bulk book purchases, contact:

G. RANDALL PUBLISHING CO.
1505 N. GROVELAND AVE.
LOGVIEW, TEXAS 75601
www.grandallpub.com
Office – (903) 753-6467
Fax – (903) 753-5788

For general information and booking for speaking engagements, contact:

Joel D. Johnson
jdjohnson@grandallpub.com

Other available books by Joel D. Johnson:
- *The American Dream is Success in a Business of Your Own.* Powerful pointers to start or "jumpstart" your business. Secrets for successful business planning.
  ISBN 0-9659439-0-9
  USA $12.50/Canada $16.00

www.ingramcontent.com/pod-product-compliance
Lightning Source LLC
Chambersburg PA
CBHW071705090426
42738CB00009B/1675